T0293672

PRAISE FOR *THE DIRECT TO CONSUMER PLAYBOOK*

'Very few books are both as inspiring and useful as this. Mike Stevens has looked beyond the glossy case histories to the real learning curves of success and failure in DTC and feeds the flame of our entrepreneurial spirit as he does so.'

Adam Morgan, author of *Eating the Big Fish* and Founder and Partner of Eatbigfish

'I loved reading the gritty backstory of so many of my favourite founders and brands. Mike Stevens really brings it all together concisely and compellingly. Chock full of helpful learnings – a must-read for anyone adventuring and playing in the DTC world.'

Jonathan Petrides, Founder and CEO of allplants

'Finally, a book taking on the DTC world. Recommended.'

Alessandro Savelli, Founder and MD of Pasta Evangelists

'Packed full of inspirational stories from pioneering brands, this book will prove a treasure trove of insight and learning for everyone who is interested in the DTC space.'

Simon Duffy MBE, Founder of Bulldog Skincare and Waken Mouthcare

'An essential read for those who work in DTC or are thinking about setting up on their own. The case studies and interviews with some of the UK's fastest growing DTC scaleups brilliantly capture the common challenges and different approaches to meeting them.'

Aron Gelbard, Founder and CEO of Bloom & Wild

'A must-read for anybody working in marketing. DTC is so much more than a sales channel, and Mike Stevens's book provides a healthy dose of case study inspiration and best practice tips around where brand meets e-commerce.'

Mark Palmer, Former Green & Black's and Pret A Manger Marketing Director and Founder of Cawston Press

'The book I wish I had when starting Heights (and knew very little about the space). No matter where you are on your journey, there's always more to learn, but Mike Stevens has done a great job of distilling everything we need to know in one superb book. A must-read if you're serious about DTC'.

Dan Murray-Setter, Co-founder of Heights and Host of the UK's top business podcast, 'Secret Leaders'

'Mike Stevens has drawn together the hard-earned lessons of the UK's most successful DTC companies, unearthing what it really took to make them fly. This book gives you the insights you just can't get elsewhere.'

Jon Wright, Partner at JamJar Investments and Co-founder of innocent drinks

'A fantastic insight into some of the most successful DTC brands out there.'

Oliver Bridge, Founder of Cornerstone

'Running a fast-growth business is all about learning. You often learn from your own mistakes, but it's far, far better to learn from others, from those that have gone before you and paved the way. Mike Stevens has done an incredible job assembling an all-star cast for us all to learn from and has presented their lessons in a truly engaging way. A must-read for all entrepreneurs.'

Guy Blaskey, Founder and CEO of Pooch & Mutt

'Companies can and should make the world a better place and win the hearts of people. This book, like its author, is guiding you to dare to be outspoken, different, better and more fact-based. Learn how to open pathways for loyal brand advocates to join you on your mission.'
Henk Jan Beltman, Chief Chocolate Officer at Tony's Chocolonely

'DTC is the most important emerging tool for anyone who makes a physical product. However, it is also the most misunderstood. Mike Stevens has captured the spirit of the DTC landscape while also highlighting just what this channel can do.'
Anthony Fletcher, former CEO of graze and Founder of I Believe in Science

'I guess you could call me a data-driven marketing native and I grew up in an extended family of small local retailers, so I was really excited to read this new book about the direct to consumer phenomenon. Mike Stevens has an accessible style – it's easy to dip in and out of the founders' stories and you really feel like you're eavesdropping on Stevens's conversations with them. These entrepreneurs generously share their DTC experiences, good and bad, including Snag's data-driven strategy, Huel's focus on price point, and Tails's obsession with customer connection. I particularly liked the chapter summaries, which made me stop and think, "Should I do that?" Essential reading for anyone who works in or for the direct to consumer world.'
Mark Runacus MBE, Co-founder of Wax/On

'I'm so glad this book exists! What a fantastic insight into how businesses are really built. It's never pretty and it's not simple, but could anything be more fun? Mike Stevens has captured the stark reality of what it's really like being at the vanguard of DTC. I wish I'd had this book when I started Snag.'
Brie Read, CEO and Founder of Snag Group

'Mike Stevens's book is a goldmine of hard-earned lessons and priceless insight from some of the most inspiring, disruptive and successful DTC brands of the last few years. It's a must-read for any entrepreneur looking to start or scale their DTC channel.'
Jason Gibb, Founder of Bread & Jam Festival for food entrepreneurs

'Mike Stevens packs every useful lesson about building and scaling DTC companies into a single, digestible book. Bringing each to life through engaging case studies and interviews with the people who are building graze, Heights, Bloom & Wild, Ugly Drinks and many others. If you're thinking about launching a consumer product startup or are involved in them in any way, this is required reading.'
Damian Routley, Chief Commercial Officer of Founders Factory

'OMG, get the DTC Playbook ASAP.'
Mike Coulter, Creative Director of The Do Lectures

The Direct to Consumer Playbook

The stories and strategies of the brands that wrote the DTC rules

Mike Stevens

KoganPage

First published in Great Britain and the United States in 2022 by Kogan Page Limited

2nd Floor, 45 Gee Street	8 W 38th Street, Suite 902	4737/23 Ansari Road
London	New York, NY 10018	Daryaganj
EC1V 3RS	USA	New Delhi 110002
United Kingdom		India

www.koganpage.com

Kogan Page books are printed on paper from sustainable forests.

ISBNs

Hardback	978 1 3986 0544 2
Paperback	978 1 3986 0542 8
Ebook	978 1 3986 0543 5

British Library Cataloguing-in-Publication Data

A CIP record for this book is available from the British Library.

Library of Congress Cataloging-in-Publication Data

Names: Stevens, Mike, 1951-author.
Title: The direct to consumer playbook: the stories and strategies of the
   brands that wrote the DTC rules edition / Mike Stevens.
Description: London, United Kingdom; New York, NY: Kogan Page Limited,
   2022. | Includes bibliographical references and index.
Identifiers: LCCN 2022005147 (print) | LCCN 2022005148 (ebook) | ISBN
   9781398605428 (paperback) | ISBN 9781398605442 (hardback) | ISBN
   9781398605435 (ebook)
Subjects: LCSH: Direct marketing. | Consumers' preferences. | Branding
   (Marketing)
Classification: LCC HF5415.126 .S74 2022 (print) | LCC HF5415.126 (ebook)
   | DDC 658.8/72–dc23/eng/20220207
LC record available at https://lccn.loc.gov/2022005147
LC ebook record available at https://lccn.loc.gov/2022005148

Typeset by Integra Software Services, Pondicherry
Print production managed by Jellyfish
Printed and bound by CPI Group (UK) Ltd, Croydon CR0 4YY

For anyone brave enough to try. Godspeed.

CONTENTS

ABOUT THE AUTHOR

Mike Stevens is a UK-based entrepreneur, passionate about consumer packaged goods and challenger brands. Mike learnt his trade in the early 2000s as part of the startup team at innocent drinks and, from there, he co-founded, built, scaled and sold his own brand, Peppersmith, the good-for-you confectionery company.

Since selling Peppersmith, he writes, consults, advises and is a mentor for the next wave of challenger brands shaking up what came before.

He lives with his wife and two sons by the sea.

Please say hi at:

Twitter: twitter.com/openmikestevens

LinkedIn: www.linkedin.com/in/mikejstevens

Website: www.stevens.earth

KEY TERMS

Like most industries, DTC has its fair share of jargon and acronyms. While I have tried to keep things simple and explain things as we go, during the interviews or when trying to specify, this book has plenty of examples of DTC speak.

To help set you up to enjoy the book and enable you to chat like a DTC veteran, here are some of the most common terms and acronyms you will come across.

DTC: direct to consumer

DTC is the method of selling products directly to the end consumers without using intermediaries like wholesalers or retailers. DTC has always been around. However, the introduction of the internet to facilitate transactions and reach customers means it is now possible to run DTC channels at a scale previously unseen.

CAC: customer acquisition cost

CAC is the amount you spend to acquire one customer. CAC is usually calculated by your total marketing spend divided by the number of customers gained. With the right level of data available, it is possible to work out your CAC for different channels or campaigns.

LTV: lifetime value

The LTV is the value (usually a forecast or prediction) of the total amount of profit a single customer will bring to a business. Correctly calculating LTV will enable you to determine your marketing budgets and cash flow requirements.

CPG: consumer packaged goods

CPGs are anything made for consumers to buy and use directly that require regular replacement or replenishment. Examples include food and drink, household goods, beauty products and clothes. **FMCG** is a variation on CPG, which means fast-moving consumer goods, and is generally applied to products replenished daily or weekly and are relatively low cost, e.g. groceries.

MVP: minimum viable product

An MVP is the most basic version of the product with just enough features to be useable by customers. MVPs are designed to test the feasibility and attractiveness of a product and are usually rapidly iterated until suitable for more general adoption.

VC: venture capital

A VC firm is a professional investment organization that typically provides finance for startups and fast-growing businesses. Equity is exchanged for investment with the expectation that the VC will sell that equity at a profit in the future. In early-stage companies, investments usually are for a minority stake. However, in more mature businesses, a VC might take a majority or even total ownership, hoping they will make a profit at a later date.

Angel and pre-seed round

These investments are generally smaller investments at a very early stage from family, friends and business angels. Business angels typically are high net worth individuals who invest their own capital into young businesses. These individuals would normally have a background in the industries they support.

Seed-round

Typically pre-revenue investments to provide the capital required to bring a product or service to market. Unlike most Angel and pre-seed rounds, seed rounds can attract institutional investment.

Series A

The business would have proven itself at this stage, and more significant investments are made to scale the business. Further investment rounds to grow the company can follow designated Series B, Series C, Series D, etc.

Equity crowdfunding

Equity crowdfunding allows individuals to invest in companies in exchange for equity. These investments are typically for smaller amounts but can be combined with more significant investments from institutional funds or business angels.

AOV: average order value

The average order size per customer.

PPC: pay per click

Digital marketing where advertisers will pay a fee each time one of their ads is clicked.

CTR: click-through rate

The CTR refers to how often people click on a link you've provided. This measure is crucial for measuring the effectiveness of email marketing and website design.

ROI: return on investment

The ROI is the measure of how well an activity or investment has performed. ROI is calculated by the benefit (gain) divided by the cost of the investment.

ROAS: return on advertising spend

Like ROI, the ROAS is the return gained from an investment; however, in this instance, it refers solely to the investment into digital advertising.

TAM: total addressable market

TAM is the total revenue opportunity available for a product or service.

DNVB: a digitally native vertical brand

A DNVB is a DTC company that has been born on the internet and has complete control of its supply chain and customer experience. DNVB may evolve into an omnichannel company later on; however, they will have established their brand reputation via their DTC channel.

Omnichannel

Omnichannel is a sales strategy that tries to meet the customer wherever they are. An omnichannel brand will look to serve you whether you are on their website, on a marketplace (e.g. Amazon), in-store or in other locations such as gyms and restaurants. Multichannel is similar to omnichannel; however, it is more limited and does not try to connect with the customer everywhere but instead focuses on more channels.

Business incubator

A business incubator is an organization that helps startup companies and individual entrepreneurs to develop their businesses by providing support and access to services they need to grow.

Introduction

How the potential of direct-to-consumer
sales revealed itself to me

In 2009, my co-founder, Dan Shrimpton, asked me if we should create a webshop for our new confectionery brand, Peppersmith. Just eight months before, we had quit our jobs to start our company, which we hoped was about to turn the confectionery industry on its head. My previous job was being part of the startup team at the legendary smoothie company innocent drinks. I had met Dan at innocent before he had gone on to work at the branding agency Jones Knowle Ritchie. We knew how to launch a new food and drink product and had chosen to shake up the confectionery category. We decided on confectionery because it was a category stuck in the past. The incumbent products were full of chemicals and sugar despite the prevailing trends for more natural, healthy and sustainable products. Our solution was the world's first all-natural and good-for-you chewing gum. And by the end of 2009, we were getting ready to launch.

Like most products at the time, we were designed to be a retail brand, with e-commerce as an afterthought. Our website was a place to show off our brand and share our thoughts. We had no ambitions for it to directly generate any revenue. So when Dan asked me if we should add on some sort of e-commerce capability, my response was a shrugged 'I guess so'.

Our challenge as a new startup was that it would take time for us to get our products into your local supermarket or corner shop. The reality of the retail industry is that even if you have a good product and the supermarkets and retail chains want to put it into their ranges, it can take many months or even years to get it on the shelf. So I thought that allowing customers to order products when they couldn't find us in their local store seemed like a sensible idea. I imagined someone living in a little village just outside Aberdeen, hearing about Peppersmith for the first time and wanting to try the product.

Enabling e-commerce

By adding a webshop to our website, we knew that there was a chance, if we could encourage customers to look us up on the internet, they might also buy our products online. As chewing gum was the sort of item you picked up on impulse and typically did not buy in bulk, our expectations for online sales were low. However, it remained an opportunity to capture lost sales for the super keen while the retailers caught up. In addition, anybody could now try the product as soon as they heard about us. So we did not have to worry about them forgetting they had ever seen us before, if and when the brand eventually appeared in store.

To set up our webshop, we found a little bolt-on tool for our WordPress website, called Prestashop (this was before Shopify became ubiquitous). It meant we could add a 'buy now' button and use PayPal as a payment option. Because we only made one product at the start, it was easy enough to set up a 'buy now' product page, fix a price and configure some shipping rules. In next to no time, we had a fully functioning webshop for our new natural chewing gum product.

Providing a platform for growth

Having a webshop when we launched turned out to be a smart move. We were getting some great PR. Journalists and bloggers were publishing positive write-ups and reviews far more quickly than we were getting meetings with the big retailers. So having a webshop allowed us to make those first crucial sales while the retailers had yet to catch on. Things really took off in February 2010, a month after launch, when Peppersmith featured in an emailed newsletter called the *DailyCandy*. Based out of New York, in 2010, it was 'the' list of the best new boutiques, restaurants and products from around the world. It also had a subscriber reach of 2.5 million trend-setting early adopters.

Immediately after our appearance in the *DailyCandy*, website hits shot up, as did online orders. We sold tens of thousands of packs. Of course, being a UK business, most orders were domestic, but there was also plenty of international interest. We'd even noticed some celebrity names among all the sticky labels we printed off, which only added to the excitement. Getting the orders was fantastic, but we then had to live up to our side of the bargain and get the stock out the door and delivered. The operational part was no easy task. We had to sort through the requests, print out the labels, find the right-sized boxes, write the shipping notes, pick and pack up the orders before eventually hauling packages down to the local post office.

The *DailyCandy* was our first experience of the power of digital marketing. Furthermore, we soon realized we could now chat with our new customers directly, as we had all their email addresses. We were also learning a lot about the logistics of sending our products through the post. However, despite all the weekly brown tape, sticky labels and cardboard boxes, the truth was, we didn't yet properly understand the opportunity of selling online. So our focus remained on getting Peppersmith into shops, and we were slowly getting better at that.

We started selling in big-name UK retailers like Sainsbury's, Waitrose, Boots, Holland & Barrett, WH Smith and Whole Foods Market. We were also in thousands of independent stockists up and down the country. The problem was that while this sounds like success, these listings were a drop in the ocean. For most people, it was still a challenge to find us in-store. Most retailers were yet to be convinced that they should add Peppersmith to their range, and for that reason alone, we kept the webshop ticking over. After all, every sale was important for our young business.

Then it happened again.

This time it was a two-page article in *The Times* newspaper, explaining the health benefits of our main ingredient, xylitol. In addition to giving a glowing endorsement to our core ingredient, it also recommended Peppersmith as a great way to access the health benefits. There was even a product shot and a link to our website. The coverage was brilliant – you couldn't buy this type of publicity (we know because we'd tried). The impact was even more dramatic than the initial batch of PR we had.

When the article hit, Dan and I were in Amsterdam at a coffee retailer event. We were trying to cosy up to the likes of Starbucks and Costa Coffee and convince them that they needed Peppersmith gum and mints in their shops. One wet Wednesday morning, we got a call from Gracie, our marketing manager, asking what we'd done as the phone hadn't stopped ringing since she stepped in the office. We had no idea about the press mention. No one had told us it was coming. But, as well as the phone ringing off the hook, it was obvious something big was happening as email orders kept appearing in the inbox.

'Get yourself back here and order some more stock into the office' was the last thing Gracie said to me as we cut short our coffee shop dreams and jumped on the next flight back to London.

The online orders kept coming – both on our webshop and on Amazon. Amazon had recently started selling food, and we were one of the first products offered on the UK platform. We spent the next few weeks speedily shipping orders from the office and making sure both ourselves and Amazon didn't run out of stock.

When the dust settled, we started to look at the numbers. We'd had, by far, our biggest ever month in sales and, encouragingly, online order rates remained higher than they'd been before the *Times* article appeared – our retention rates were good, not that we knew what that meant at the time.

To our frustration, despite the increased awareness, some of the retail sales were still bumpy, with the problem being the ability for retailers to adapt. The PR had stimulated demand both online and in the bricks and mortar outlets, but it wasn't long before we started noticing stock problems with the retailers. Their systems couldn't react quickly enough to the increase in demand, which led to empty spaces on shelves where our stock should be. We also naively thought the positive PR and sustained new demand would finally convince those remaining retailers to list Peppersmith. No such luck.

It was 2013, and the retail sector was struggling. Tesco was just about to become embroiled in a supplier payments scandal. However, Tesco wasn't the only one facing difficulties. All the other UK supermarket chains were seeing a decline in profits. Changing customer habits and the rise of internet shopping meant the success they had been enjoying for decades was now a thing of the past. These once healthy businesses were looking for ways to cuts costs to stay afloat. Critically, for a small challenger brand like us, retailers were becoming less interested in incorporating new products and suppliers. Instead, they were downsizing head office staff, which led to smaller, overstretched buying teams. The need for quick profits and increased efficiency meant retailers were focusing their time more and more on the larger established suppliers. Reduced buyer resources combined with the power of the bigger brands had resulted in the maintenance of the status quo. So despite our marketing successes, new listings were even harder to unlock.

It was not all bad. We still had some great stockists and were slowly adding more. However, at the same time, as retail started getting harder and harder, we had seen organically, and whenever we had any marketing breakthroughs, online was increasingly where the action was. This moment was the tipping point. Retail was gruelling, and direct to consumer (DTC) sales presented a better, more practicable and engaging way of serving our customers. We needed to figure out the rules of DTC.

Establishing the rules of the game

By 2015 the DTC business model had been well established. Warby Parker, Casper and Dollar Shave Club were making waves in the US, and graze, Pact Coffee and Gymshark were doing the same in the UK. From being innovators, we were now playing catch-up. We started asking ourselves many questions, including what's the best website platform? What's the best way to accept payments? What can we do to improve the online and delivery experience? How much money should we put into advertising on Facebook? Or should it be Twitter, Instagram or Google? Can we sell both on our website and Amazon, or do we need to choose? Will retailers get upset with us as we try to serve more customers directly? How can we save postage costs? How best do we follow up with new customers? Should we outsource customer service? It was a long list.

To find answers, I started asking my founder peer group for the best DTC strategies for a food and drink brand. I discovered two things: (1) there is quite a bit to think about, and (2) nobody knew all the answers. Like us, they were figuring it out on the job.

Initial conversations about DTC were fun and enlightening. We were told that graze was saving postage costs by having a box under 25 mm in height. I had a few drinks with the Cafe Pod coffee company while they talked me through the basics of lifetime value (LTV) and customer acquisition costs (CAC). The theory was if your CAC<LTV, then spend as much as possible on CAC and make DTC your profit-making engine. It sounded simple in principle, but digital marketing was just like every other sort of marketing – complicated and expensive. What's more, we had no way of adequately measuring Lifetime Value.

We experimented with all sorts of marketing activities, most of which did not work. One of our biggest lessons was not to waste money on a pay per click (PPC) agency. A PPC agency offered the promise of getting maximum returns on your Google AdWords spend. However, we found that while these agencies may have understood how Google's advertising algorithm worked, they had little appreciation of what a positive return on investment looked like for a company making a physical product. We found that they typically only think about digital marketing spend and revenue and forget that, unlike with a software service, you also have to pay to make the product and ship it to your customers.

By now, we had redesigned our website with DTC sales as a primary objective. Out went the free software to be replaced by a Shopify subscription. Next, we found a warehouse that would take care of the packing and shipping for us – packing up boxes and dragging them down to the post office became a distant memory. Critically, we also started to consider the reasons why our customers were ordering from us directly. We needed to find out if there was enough demand to get a return on any investment of time and money we spent on our DTC service.

My frustrations with accessing best practice

I wanted to learn and learn quickly. Leaning on my network of fellow founders was helpful, but we needed to know more. We toyed with bringing in an e-commerce specialist but couldn't afford to do that. We were going to have to continue to figure it out for ourselves. In the hope of finding a shortcut, I jumped on Amazon to buy a 'How to Set up E-commerce for Your Brand' type book. I was surprised to find out one didn't seem to exist. I knew DTC was a relatively new concept, but it was also something that most CPG (consumer packaged goods) brands were now trying to figure out.

Fast forward four years, and we'd managed to build a large chunk of our business from our DTC efforts. About a third of the revenues were now generated online. We were processing thousands of online orders each month, with Amazon also doing similar volumes. Traditional bricks and mortar sales had also grown and still made up most of our revenues, but our DTC channel was now a significant part of our business. DTC sales were also where we could be the most creative and gave me the most pleasure. In addition to being profitable, the real joy was that we were constantly interacting with our most loyal and enthusiastic customers via our DTC sales. I loved it, but I was still a DTC white belt and remained baffled that DTC best practice was still relatively hard to find.

Time to move on

Peppersmith was growing and profitable, but it still needed significant funding to help it compete with the giant confectionery companies that continued to dominate the category. We received investment offers; however, they all had their catches. We'd also received an offer from someone who didn't want to invest but wanted to buy the company. The amount tabled would not make us rich, but it was something we needed to consider. Finally, after some soul searching, we agreed that it was the right time to sell the business. Unlike DTC, there are plenty of books written about doing this – you should read them. It's a rollercoaster.

Having come through the other side of a business exit and now having stepped away from Peppersmith, I noticed there was a book still missing from my bookshelf. And that was the DTC playbook for brands. It was still unwritten, and I realized the task of creating it had fallen to me. I had the experience, access to a great network of founders and now had the time.

I set myself on a new quest – to find out how to properly set up and run a DTC business guided by the very best. This book is the result of that search.

What to expect from this book

This book contains 15 chapters of 16 case studies of the best and most influential brands and DTC practitioners. The brands I spoke to sell various products, including flowers, frozen food, sodas, tights, razors, toiletries, clothes, toilet rolls, paint and supplements. The commonality is that they all make branded physical products and are famous for building successful and sustainable DTC businesses. Of those 16, 12 are from the UK, three from the US and one from Australia. Their locations are more for reference than anything else as the basic rules for doing DTC tend to be the same whether you are from Birmingham, Berlin, Boston or Buenos Aires.

From these case studies, you hear from the founders (plus one CEO) how their backgrounds and experiences led them to success. I have done my best to capture the words and spirit of this unique bunch of individuals. Wherever possible, I have just let the founders themselves recount their stories and explain why they made their choices in their own words. Every story is different, as is every founder; however, you will see a common thread of the desire to solve problems and better serve the needs of their customers.

What this book is not is a step-by-step 101 guide to e-commerce. There are other books, YouTube videos, Twitter threads and blog posts that will show you how to configure a webshop, take payments, set up a Facebook advertising campaign and help you work out your margins. So if you need that sort of help, don't stop reading but understand this book won't give you all the technical answers. This book is not an instruction manual in the sense that you can simply follow the rules and replicate the outcomes. If only being an entrepreneur is that easy. This book is about inspiration and wisdom.

The reason I have chosen not to detail the more technical tactics is that they are ephemeral. As you will see as you read the book, the DTC landscape is evolving at lightning speed. For example, advising you to spend money on Facebook ads rather than brand collaborations will result in this book rapidly becoming outdated. Even today's leading platforms like Shopify and Instagram will be upgraded and then likely be usurped by newer and better tools. The book is not just what you should do but also explains why you should do it.

I've taken these 16 inspirational brand stories and focused on those fundamental choices each company made, which fuelled their success. Concentrating on the foundational strategies and the startup stories should mean this book will remain informative and entertaining whether you are reading it in 2022 or a decade later.

I have written this book primarily for anyone looking to start or improve their own DTC business. For that reason, there's a summary of the most critical take-outs at the end of each case study. These are the lessons each founder has been generous enough to share. Please apply these lessons to your own endeavours, experimenting and iterating as you go. Then please pay it forward and share your learnings with the next generation of startup founders.

In the same way as the tools and tactics are forever changing, so are the companies that make the DTC landscape so vibrant and exciting. The 16 businesses I have chosen will undoubtedly have changed shape by the time you read this. A month in DTC is a year in the old-fashioned world of retailer reliant consumer goods. Most of the companies featured should have continued to grow. Many will now be offering additional products and services. Some may have been acquired by ambitious VCs or even the bigger, more traditional brands who still influence our retail choices. Those companies who set the consumer goods rules decades ago are now scrambling to capture the value that the new generation of challengers have created and are often ready to pay big as they try and catch up. Lastly, some of the founders might have moved on to begin new adventures.

Whatever happens to these businesses, consider their founding stories. That these companies and their creators have had the opportunities to grow, scale and become better versions of themselves is due to their origins and their initial choices.

How I uncovered the stories and strategies of the best in class DTC brands

I sat with the founders for many hours in each interview. Sometimes in-person and sometimes on a video call. The video calls were necessary as I wrote this book during the strange times of the COVID-19 global pandemic. So while it was disappointing that I could not meet everyone in real life, the timing was such that e-commerce was also going through its most extensive period of growth and getting DTC right was more important than ever before.

My questions were driven by my curiosity and the frustrations I faced when building my own DTC operation. You will find the answers carry an incredible amount of wisdom and knowledge; they'd been there, done it, stumbled, tried again and eventually worked it out.

I also make no apologies for writing enthusiastically about the brands in the book. They are the companies and products that are slowly but surely making us all a little bit happier, and often healthier. Most are also progressive when considering the external social impacts of being a manufactured good and are doing their bit to ensure our consumption habits do not irrecoverably wreck the planet. None of the products or brands are perfect, but they are successful because they are better and more relevant than what has come before. They are the best in class. I share in their desire to innovate, invent and improve. I hope you do too.

There is no requirement to read the chapters in order. Instead, pick the companies and products that interest you the most. Then go back and read the others to cross-reference and see how each case study reinforces the others.

Everyone I interviewed was extremely generous in sharing their stories and what they have learned along the way. Please use this shared knowledge and experience to inform your future business endeavours and specifically help and inspire you to build your own DTC empires.

I hope you enjoy reading the stories as much as I did writing them. Finally, I hope this is the book that has been missing from your bookshelf and means it is now easier to build on the shoulders of these DTC pioneers.

01

In the beginning was graze.com

graze

When Dan and I started Peppersmith in 2009, we had a road map. Between us, we had spent 14 years at innocent, one of the most successful UK food and drink start-ups in the last few decades. We had seen how to do it; find a category to disrupt, develop a high-quality product and brand, and convince supermarkets and wholesalers to stock it. Marketing would be done in-store and, if we could afford it, using print and media. This roadmap was the world we knew, and while it was never going to be easy, we felt very little pressure to follow a different path.

A few miles down the road from our office in Putney, there was a company that was playing by a different set of rules. It did not take us long to become aware of graze, who launched about a year before us. They were different. While the rest of the food and drink start-up world, including us, were zigging, they were zagging. It seemed that everything they did was unique. They were a new snack brand, but they were not in the shops. Instead, they were selling their products using a DTC subscription model. What's more, rather than outsourcing production, they had their own factory. Also, unlike us, who made just a couple of products, they were making dozens and were adding more to their portfolio each week.

While we were haggling with the UK's biggest retailers, graze did their own thing and were succeeding. By the time we had hit our first million, they already had £40 million of sales with over 100,000 weekly subscribers. It seemed that they were three steps ahead of the rest of us and operating in a different world. I was a fanboy. I desperately wanted to know how they achieved these results and see if I could incorporate any of their strategies into my business. It was becoming an obsession, and that obsession became the genesis for this book. What was it about DTC that was better than the traditional launch model we were using? And if it was a better model, what did you have to do to get it right?

While I was trying to figure out the mysteries of DTC, graze became one of the UK's biggest snack brands and was eventually acquired by Unilever in a nine-figure deal in 2019. Their success had proved that DTC needed to be taken seriously. Therefore graze was the natural place to start my odyssey to understand DTC brands and what they did differently from companies like mine. Hence my interview with graze CEO Anthony Fletcher was the first for this book. I had a lot to learn. Fortunately, he was happy to walk me through the story.

Why being industry outsiders was an advantage

One of the reasons graze were so different was that they were started by experts in technology and logistics and not in food. So what could have been a weakness was actually a strength. Freed from any preconceptions, they thought differently from the rest of the industry.

The foundations for the graze method can be traced back to another pioneering UK business, LoveFilm. LoveFilm was the UK's answer to the first, pre-streaming, iteration of Netflix. LoveFilm was a business that sent DVDs through the post, thus saving you the hassle and the late fees of getting your DVD rentals from your local Blockbuster. Graham Bosher was a co-founder at LoveFilm, and when he left the business during its acquisition by Amazon, he turned his gaze to new opportunities. It did not take long for him to identify the snacking category as the next target to use his experience of tech, logistics and brand building.

The new business was to be similar to LoveFilm, i.e. subscription products through the post, but instead of DVDs, they would send snacks instead. A DTC model had never been tried at scale in the snacking industry before. Snacks were all about immediate satisfaction. What's more, the products were cheap, making the relative delivery costs high. Despite this, Graham had planned to offer a variety of low-cost, healthy snacks delivered to your door, or more often than not, to your office desk. As this was all new and untested, they had some fundamental challenges to overcome, such as how they package and send out their products, what snacks are best, how to find customers willing to subscribe and how to keep the costs down. The list turned out to be quite long and, according to Anthony, led many would-be investors and industry veterans to describe the business model as 'bonkers'.

The outsider status of the founding team resulted in a contrarian approach that most dismissive food industry professionals were quick to reject. They failed to see graze was years ahead of its time, and the way they were doing business would soon become the envy of the industry. Not so, Anthony, who was one of the first food and drink insiders to take what graze was trying to do seriously and was getting very excited about it.

At the time, Anthony was innovation manager at innocent, responsible for new product development and market entry strategies. He was getting restless and toyed with starting his own food business. 'I was annoying the hell out of my wife, tampering with all sorts of food and drink ideas at home in our kitchen, when I came across graze,' explained Anthony.

> It wasn't just a brand idea; it was also a new business model that intrigued me. So I got my job at graze by going down and knocking on the door, saying that I had been at innocent and thought graze was the next innocent drinks and a really big and exciting idea.

Using data to drive every decision

Graze had been in operation for about a year when Anthony joined, initially as their marketing manager. He quickly discovered that one of the main differences between a traditional fast-moving consumer goods (FMCG) brand and a DTC company was the importance of data and something called performance marketing.

> I think the easiest way to explain performance marketing is that as soon as you are an online business, there is a huge amount of additional information available to you. And this gives you new strategies in terms of how you invest in traffic, building a brand, how your website looks. It completely changes the visibility of your marketing metrics and the way you can go about marketing.

In its simplest form, performance marketing is using your online data to make better decisions more quickly. Leaning forward to emphasize his feelings on this further, Anthony went on, 'I would argue that if you want to scale an online business, sooner or later you will have to master performance marketing.'

Anthony discovered graze was a business built around the data it collected. He also found an operating model that was flexible enough to adapt to what that data was telling them. From the start, customers were able to rate the different products they received. These ratings made it easy to see which products their customers enjoyed and which needed to be redeveloped or scrapped. For example, one of the things graze did in their early days was to send fruit out to their customers. However, the data and the customer service emails quickly let them know that fruit in the post is not a great idea. Anthony explained:

> At the time, the solution [to fixing the product problem] was unusual. But because we are an online business, it was easy to iterate and try out new things. The amazing thing about graze is that it wasn't one of those businesses which started with an amazing product; it was the business model which helped the business discover what were the relevant and right quality products that people wanted.

The advantages of keeping operations in-house

Being nimble with their product range was one of the main reasons they had built their production facility. Most start-up food and drink brands tend to outsource their manufacturing and buy time and expertise from existing producers to make their products. The advantages of outsourcing are low capital requirements, flexibility to grow, smaller production runs and access to accredited and audited equipment and processes. The significant downside is that it is much harder to do something completely new. It only usually makes sense for a factory to sell more of what it already does. If you are trying to reinvent the wheel, it is much harder to source your products from others. If you are to be unique, you will inevitability need to do it yourself.

Using the credibility Bosher had acquired through his experience and success with LoveFilm, he raised enough seed capital to handpick a founding team, create a brand, build a dedicated production and packing facility and conceive a new relationship with the Post Office. One of the major operational constraints was to make their packaging small enough to qualify as a 'large letter' rather than a parcel, thus significantly reducing their postage costs. As no one could do this for them, they assembled their own production, packing and warehousing. As a result, they had become what is now known as vertically integrated.

Vertically integrated organizations do as much as possible in-house. The advantage of doing this is gaining total autonomy and control of their operational processes, including sourcing, manufacturing, logistics and customer orders. Vertically integrated supply chains are now popular with many DTC brands whose products are significantly different from industry standards. It also gives these companies total responsiveness and the ability to innovate rapidly. The other benefit is that every cost driver is known and controlled. Knowing exactly how much something costs to make is critical to getting your margins to work.

Anthony explained the advantages:

> Having our own factory was something that most start-up brands did not have. The big difference for us is that we could deeply understand our products and how they are made. This knowledge allowed us to invest in innovation in a very different way. We used data to tell us what to change. We now have over half a billion reviews which we use to make better products.

The power of performance marketing

As well as using data to improve on their products, data is also critical to finding and retaining customers.

> When it came to generating demand, this is where performance
> marketing came in. It needed to help us work out how to get people to
> try this new concept, which many people thought of as a bonkers idea.
> So we used performance marketing to work out how we get people to
> try the snacks and how much it costs to do so. There are two metrics
> to think about: 'Acquisition Cost' and 'Lifetime Value'. You can fairly
> quickly calculate how much it costs for each new visit and conversion
> on the website. Then after several years of purchasing habits, you can
> very accurately work out if you make money on that investment.

One of the problems you have with any new DTC business is that while it is relatively easy to measure the customer acquisition cost, broader assumptions are required to calculate lifetime value. When asked how you manage this, Anthony's view was:

> You need to decide how you want to run your business; do you want
> to start quickly acquiring customers at a cost which might not be
> supported by the lifetime value but achieve lots of growth and trial. Or
> do you want to be more conservative and manage your cash until the
> situation becomes more clear? Getting this wrong is the main reason
> many DTC start-up businesses go bust.

The intense focus on numbers and data has been one of the reasons for graze's success.

> One of the things which really helped us was our attitude to data. Very
> early on in the business, we put a lot of effort into how data was stored
> and how it could be accessed. It wasn't just performance marketing. It
> was everything from finance data, product review data, any data that
> could help our customer service team respond to queries. It helped that
> we have a pretty geeky company culture.

The importance of looking beyond your own data

While recording, storing, analysing and making good decisions using data has significantly contributed to their success, Anthony was also keen to point out that it is still possible to get things wrong even with all this information. For example, in 2013, when launching in the United States, they used data to quickly test their assumptions, refine their products and figure out the best marketing techniques for a new market. However, the challenges that caused the most problems in the United States came externally, from the macro general market trends and what their competitors were doing. This information was not obvious from their internal data.

'When it came to our US launch, I think we got one thing absolutely right and one thing wrong,' explained Anthony.

> The thing we got right was the minimum viable product test we did. We took about eight weeks to make a US website and actually launched nationally. We measured over 100 KPIs [key performance indicators] for eight weeks to understand all sorts of things. This data was incredibly useful in flushing out what were the real issues of going into the US market, and it turned out some of the things we thought would be a problem were not. For example, we thought portion size would be a big issue for us, but it was clear via the MVP [minimum viable product] process that the US consumer appreciated that it was a good size for the product. At the same time, it was clear that the US market did not understand our British colloquialisms. For example, they didn't understand what mango chutney was and thought it was a grim acidic lump of yellow goo and not a tasty condiment. It taught us that we quickly needed to adapt the product range for that market. The challenge and the thing we did not anticipate came from the fact that the US market was also evolving at the same time graze had entered the market. We were guilty of not paying enough attention to the competition and what they were doing, which in hindsight is a natural thing for a traditional retail brand as you are on the shelf against the competition. We were too internally focused and were a bit slow to react. The market was moving rather than the consumer moving, and

it was hard for us to adapt to these market-led challenges rather than more the operational ones.

Graze eventually ended its US DTC service in 2019 when Unilever acquired the business.

Reaching beyond DTC and going multichannel

Graze are a trailblazing business that does things first. Initially, they did DTC when everyone else was trying to launch in retail. They had a factory when everyone else outsourced. They launched in the United States when it was more typical for US brands to expand into the UK and Europe. They then did something that at the time felt equally as radical. In 2015, after establishing themselves as the go-to DTC snack brand, graze surprised everybody. They went multichannel. Multichannel means graze are no longer a pure-play DTC business. Now they also sell their products in traditional bricks and mortar retail stores and supermarkets. At the time, it seemed an unusual thing to do. After all, they were different and better because they were a DTC company. However, it is now a common model for DTC brands to start direct, then once they are established also begin to sell their products into traditional retail and wholesale channels. Likewise, more established retail brands are now also developing their own DTC strategies.

Anthony is a fan of this multichannel approach, explaining, 'I think the future of commerce has got to be multichannel. For one, by not considering different channels, you limit your market opportunity, but also by utilizing different channels, it gives you new ways to compete and different ways to reach your customers.' When asked what order you should do things in, Anthony was also forthright.

I think you would be mad not to start online. While it can take a little time to build your brand reputation with your core consumers, it also gives you time to make sure your products are up to scratch. Retail is a very unforgiving environment, and it helps to go in with a bit of a reputation and a product you can feel confident on.

Being a DTC company built on constant iteration and using data turned out to be a huge advantage when it came to retail.

> Our retail customers were blown away when six weeks after launching our range, we showed them the data to convince them to de-list a third of the range and replace them with new products. This approach was totally radical, given the normal NPD cycle of 24–36 months of traditional FMCG brands. The retailers were really impressed that we were able to be proactive and react so fast.

Why access to technology is getting easier

Staying ahead of the competition is a significant driver for Anthony as there is no room for complacency with more and more brands making the most of the DTC model graze has helped to establish.

> For a direct to consumer brand, nowadays, it's comparatively simple to get going. Ten years ago, you needed incredibly specialist skills and needed to build everything from the ground up. Today the major strategy used by many entrepreneurs is they take several different basic systems, which are often cloud-based, and use them to get going into that MVP phase. As a result, there are now some very capable and relatively cheap systems and products to tap into.

Today, there is no need to build your technology from scratch, unlike when graze started, and Anthony cautions against this approach.

> When businesses bring more of their technology build in-house, they often regret it in the long run. It is because you end up building a very complex technology system that is difficult to manage and service. So if you do want to bring that complexity into the business, you have to make sure it is genuinely giving you an edge.

Why your brand, purpose and product is still more important than technology

Graze is an excellent example of how a DTC model and the data it produces can be used first to disrupt and then conquer a category. However, Anthony was also keen to remind me that none of this is possible without the foundations of a strong product and brand.

> One of the reasons we have our own factory and invest in our own machinery was to ensure fantastic product quality to back up what the brand stands for. Everything starts with the product, your brand and your purpose. If that isn't there, no amount of technology is going to help you succeed.

LESSONS FROM GRAZE

1 Get the most out of your data. Focus on gathering, storing and making data available across your whole business, not just for marketing. Use consumer data to develop, test and iterate your products until you are sure you have something that your customers will want to buy again and again. While making sure you are using all your data points, don't forget to notice what is happening outside your business. What are the trends, and what are your competitors doing? Your internal numbers can't always tell you this.

2 When it comes to performance marketing, be clear on your marketing strategy and use the numbers to validate and iterate your approach. For example, are you willing to invest a lot at the start for quick customer acquisition, or will you take a more conservative approach to optimize your products and marketing?

3 If you are trying to do something very different from the rest of the market, consider bringing manufacturing in-house. It may require more capital, but the benefits of control, responsiveness and reduced development cycles can be worth it. It will help you iterate until you have got your product right. In the case of graze, at the start, the product was not perfect. But, what they had right, was a business model that enabled them to constantly refine their products until they had something their customers really loved.

4 Once you have used DTC to establish your brand consider going into multiple channels, including retail. The major advantage of getting DTC right first is that when you are ready to launch into retail more people will be aware of your brand, and you should have the confidence that your products are what the market wants. As Anthony said, retail is a very unforgiving environment. You need a solid reputation and good products to succeed. Graze were also able to impress their retail customers by using sales data to rapidly fine-tune their range.

5 Using technology can give you a massive advantage over traditional brands. What's more, that technology is more easily accessible than ever before. However, without a strong brand and high-quality products that customers want, technology alone will not allow you to succeed.

02

From a side hustle
to international stardom

Huel

Huel HQ can be found about 30 miles north-west of Central London in the ancient market town of Tring. The town is a sleepy little settlement with a lot of history, including a mention in the Doomsday Book and a railway line built under the watchful eye of Robert Stephenson, one of the grandfathers of steam locomotion. Tring station is not actually in the town and instead located over 2 miles away. The local story is that, back in the nineteenth century, the local landowners kicked up a fuss about Stephenson's plans and forced the train station away from their prime real estate around the town. The experience of the 40-minute huff up the road to get into the town from the station is a fitting start for a visit to a company like Huel. Huel is a business that believes in putting health and fitness at the top of the priority list. So why not start any visit with a brisk walk? Huel is what some people think is the future of food, health and nutrition, and as I found out, they may be right.

Julian Hearn founded Huel in the summer of 2015, and it was shortly after their launch, I first met him. When I first spotted a Facebook ad for the brand, I was immediately fascinated by what Julian was brewing. I had never seen a product like Huel before, and even very early on, it was clear that he was gaining some serious DTC momentum. I picked up the phone, called Julian, and he was gracious enough to invite me over to show me what he was trying to do.

When I first went to visit Julian, it was with the intention to learn more about the nuts and bolts of his e-commerce setup. We were starting to step up our DTC efforts at Peppersmith, and it was evident that Julian knew what he was doing regarding launching a DTC brand. I was keen to learn. While Julian was happy to share his plans and give me a few tips, even in that first meeting, it's the product itself that is the most fascinating part of his business. The product was so different from other healthy food products it seemed all a bit outlandish. Maybe it was because it was so unusual that you could tell it would work from the start. When I decided to write this book, I knew Julian, and the Huel story needed to be in it. With this in mind, I called up again, and five years on, Julian welcomed me this time into to his shiny new HQ to tell me his account of the outstanding progress that had been made since we first met in a shabby little office at the back of his old warehouse.

Hipster gruel

Huel has been described as a meal replacement, space food, the act of vomiting in reverse, the food of the future, beige gloop and memorably as 'hipster gruel' by British comedian Dave Gorman. As you may guess from these descriptions, Huel is not everybody's cup of tea, but it is beloved by a loyal army of 'Hueligans'. Cynics beware; at the time of writing, annual sales were rapidly closing on the £100 million mark.

The reason behind the mixed reaction is that it takes a bit of work to get your head around the product. Huel is a nutritionally complete meal in a powdered form. The meals are currently available in nine different flavours, including Coffee, Banana, Salted Caramel, Vanilla and Mint Chocolate. There are also varieties to cater for high-protein and gluten-free diets and even a professional version tailored to the requirements of full-time athletes. Once you have your Huel Powder, you measure it out in line with your desired calorie intake and add water to give you a healthy, quick, convenient, simple, inexpensive meal. Julian was also keen to remind me that it also ticked the megatrends of being vegan and eradicating food waste, making it a much more sustainable option than most meals.

While it caters for professional athletes, I was fascinated to learn it was not just fitness fanatics who were buying into the benefits. Julian revealed that the largest customer segment were desk workers, often in tech or creative industries. These customers are using Huel for a quick and healthy breakfast and/or lunch fix. Speed, ease and peace of mind are the key motivations.

Alongside short preparation time, Huel's main benefit is for health and fitness; however, Julian bristles at the idea of Huel being thought of as a meal replacement, a protein shake or a slimming aid. According to Julian, Huel is a reaction and an antidote to the problems caused by the way the food and drink industry make and market their products and how we as their customers end up consuming them. The main concern cited by Julian is that the conventional focus with food is on taste and texture, with health and nutrition firmly taking a back seat. Looking at food in this way is backwards in the eyes of Julian. He explains,

> good nutrition is essential; however, the right information and access to the right nutrients are so hard to find. Look at the TV chefs; they are all taste this and taste that, but they rarely talk about the nutritional makeup of their ingredients and meals. This is the case even in their cookbooks. The result of this is an epidemic of obesity, health issues and even malnourished individuals who are actually eating loads of calories.

Julian is determined to put this right.

Julian is hardcore about healthy food, and he has an intense belief about food consumption. For him, food is either functional (i.e. used to fuel the body and keep you healthy) or it is merely 'entertainment food'. He says you can have your Sunday roast, but you need to acknowledge it as entertainment food as it does not contain the optimal amount of nutrients or calories you need. Same with your Friday night takeaway. Huel is the inverse where the primary focus is on nutrition with taste important (hence all the flavours) but secondary. It is this hierarchy that, instinctively, is the main turn off for those of us who enjoy the whole experience of preparing and eating a meal even if we recognize that what we are consuming may not be the best thing for our long-term health.

The unnatural look of the product is the main reason that, while I have always been a fan of Huel, I've hesitated to sign up. Chatting to Julian, however, was enough for me to reconsider. When it comes to promoting the benefits of good health and nutrition and highlighting how hard it is to put the right stuff in your body, Julian presents a powerful case favouring a change to our eating habits. On top of this, because the product also tackles broader issues like food waste and is a low carbon alternative means it should not be sneered at by even the most committed gastronomes. It is a good solution so long as you are prepared to think differently about how you consume your daily calories.

Voucher codes and bodyhacking

Fortunately, Julian is not afraid to be different, and he also likes to turn his convictions into actions. It was this mindset that had already made him his first fortune years before Huel by founding, building and ultimately selling a voucher code website. From its inception, Julian had an instinctive feel for the retail possibilities of the internet. He started his career in the mid-1990s at MFI, at the time the UK's biggest furniture company. It was here that Julian was put into the team to build the first e-commerce offer for the brand. While MFI ultimately failed to keep up with the times (it went out of business in 2008), Julian had learnt enough about the opportunities the internet could bring to retail to go it alone.

The main appeal behind the voucher site Julian created was a business he could run from home and thus avoid the dreary commute into London each day. Julian's main objective was to spend more time with his family. At the time his wife was pregnant, and he wanted to be on hand when the baby arrived. The voucher site was a significant success. It was soon making millions in profit with just a tiny team doing the work. While it was successful, Julian was astute enough to recognize that this success could be short-lived. More and more competitors were coming into the market, threatening to dilute the advertising revenue that powered the business. With a more challenging future on his mind, he packaged up the company and sold it on.

Julian picked up the story.

> This gave me enough money to retire if I wanted. We were grounded and didn't go crazy with the money. I ended up spending loads of wonderful time with my wife and young son. The problem is there is only so much toddler TV you can watch. Most people have the problem of too much work in their work/life balance. I now had the opposite problem.

Julian had itchy feet and was looking for a side project that allowed him to flex his entrepreneurial and creative muscles without requiring him to dedicate a crazy amount of time to it.

Initially, Julian scratched this itch with a new business called Bodyhack, a fitness website designed to cut through the conflicting advice on fitness and nutrition and sell online exercise programs. These exercise plans were complete lifestyle programs. They included both exercise regimes and strict dietary instructions to follow. To test the fitness plans, Julian put himself forward as the guinea pig and, at the age of 40, went from 21 per cent body fat to 11 per cent and said he had never been in better shape. There was a snag, however. According to Julian,

> The problem was to achieve these results as well as the exercise you have to be really disciplined with your food. I was weighing every single ingredient of every meal to make sure I had exactly the right levels of nutrients and calories. Being at home, this worked well for me; however, the consistent feedback was that while people wanted the results, they just did not have the time to collect and measure out the ingredients specified. For most of our customers, their hectic lifestyles left barely enough time for the exercise. By adding on the additional time required to meet the strict dietary rules, we were asking too much. The Bodyhack programmes were too demanding to be scalable.

While Julian had hit a roadblock with the Bodyhack idea, he had uncovered a more significant unmet need. Fixing the problem of accessing the specific nutrients and ingredients for a healthy diet and doing it quickly and easily became the new focus, with the eventual solution becoming Huel. Julian teamed up with fitness coach and nutritionist James Collier to develop a prototype for Huel, which used the latest insights from sports and food science to help optimize your nutrition and make it as easy as possible to do so.

1000 true fans

The duo went through many rounds of testing, with once again Julian using himself as the test subject. Eventually, after they had a product that Julian liked and would use, they turned to the business plan. Julian wanted to start small, and he realized that so long as he had a decent enough price point, the business only needed a relatively modest number of customers to function. He explained his thinking:

> I am probably a bit weird, but not that weird, so there must be other people out there, like me, who were looking for similar products.
> My goal at this time was to have a lifestyle business. I was thinking about the Kevin Kelly concept of 1000 true fans,[1] and I realized that if 1000 people bought £45 worth of stuff a month, I would have a business turning over £500,000 a year, and I could probably manage all this from home. That would be a nice lifestyle, and that was really the concept.'

With this goal in mind, Julian set about packaging a product that people would pay £45 a month for. Julian realized for people to buy from him every month, in addition to a good product, he had to make the experience as personal and enjoyable as possible. He felt £45 a month was a lot of money, and hence he wanted to make people feel like they were getting good value. Like many DTC subscription businesses, the model only works if your customers are loyal and are happy to pay again and again for the same products.

If customers turn off their subscription after a few months, the cost to acquire new customers increases and, they would eventually run out of potential customers to convert. They had to ensure the brand was well made and sticky. With a freelance designer, Julian created the brand with its clean, understated feel, translated this onto the product and packaging and at every step making sure the end product and proposition suited a DTC model.

A DTC-friendly product meant the bag size needed to be big enough to justify a price of £45 per order. Julian had worked out he needed to reach this price point or else the relative distribution and delivery costs would be too high to enable a workable margin. Having big enough margins also allowed him to afford to incorporate a free shaker and a t-shirt in each initial order. These extra touches enhanced the experience but again only worked if they retained those customers. The good news was that their customers, who later became the Huel tribe, were happy to pay £45 to join. Being a member of the club became a badge of honour. Huel's customers were soon posting pictures on social media wearing the Huel-branded t-shirts and became brand ambassadors by fielding questions about their Huel-branded shaker sitting proudly on their desk. Eventually, the members of the tribe became known as the 'Hueligans', a name that has been embraced at Huel HQ and now even has its own fan-owned Facebook group with nearly 10,000 members, all presumably Huel customers. By wearing the t-shirt or carrying around a shaker you showed that you cared about improving your health and nutrition and that you were the type of person who embraces new and better ways of living. Becoming a Hueligan is open to anyone with an open mind, a thirst for self-improvement and who is happy to pay £45 a month for a bag of product containing 17×400 calorie meals.

Great customer service and not being a 'dick'

Despite some mixed PR at the start, mainly due to journalists not understanding the concept, word began to spread, and the orders started to flood in. The first 1000 customers were rapidly obtained, and it quickly became evident that this would be much more than a lifestyle business. The startup made £750k in revenue in its first six months. Revenues hit £6 million in its first full year, £14 million the year after, £40 million last year and in its latest financial year £72 million. The company has so far sold over 150,000,000 meals to customers from 100 countries, with the UK and United States being the most significant markets. The North American market has become so important for the business that they have established an office in New York to make sure it can deal with US customer service enquiries in real time.

The discussion about the advantage of local offices was not the first time that customer service was mentioned in our interview. Good customer service was a theme running throughout our chat. Being human and putting the customer first is ingrained throughout the company culture. Julian explains:

> It was always essential to me that we looked after our customers incredibly well. This goes right back to the early days when I hand-signed a thank you note in the first 1000 orders, to when I switched our delivery company when I began to receive complaints about the crappy delivery experience our customers were getting. It may cost a bit more, but if your customers are unhappy, they will not come back. I have two things that resonate with me; the first is to make sure customers are happy. Everyone in the company has that mindset. The second is don't be a dick and be nice. It's pretty straightforward.

There is no doubt he means it. 'Don't be a dick' is written prominently on the office wall outside the room we are sitting in. It is a proactive and playful thing to do, and I love how this must influence the behaviour of anyone fielding a customer service call or writing an email to a supplier or customer. By having it on the wall, there is no doubt you are expected to live up to this simple commandment.

When asked about marketing, characteristically, Julian had some strong views. He said his main success in driving awareness came from word of mouth, PR (both good and bad) and Facebook. From early on, Facebook was an essential channel for customer acquisition.

The Facebook 'lookalike' feature enabled Huel to build on its first 1000 fans and find more customers who were like them and would likely also appreciate the products. While Facebook is still the main channel, it is one of many that Huel now uses to drive awareness and find new customers.

Whether it is Facebook, Instagram, Google or any other, what they have in common is they are all digital. Julian explains, 'Performance marketing, which is anything paid online, is head and shoulders above offline. I really hate offline.' Indeed, traditional non-digital offline marketing seemed to be Julian's only regret. 'We have tried it all, but no one has convinced me it works,' Julian went on. 'You see an ad on the Tube, which is great, but you then don't go upstairs, find a shop and buy some Huel. I think there is a disconnect as people don't know what it is, so they are not going to engage in it.' It's a great insight for any brand that you need to advertise in the places where you are most likely to be able to quickly convert a customer. This proximity between the customer and point of purchase is why you have big-branded displays in retail stores. If you are a digital brand, then anything offline is less likely to be effective. Doing your marketing digitally also gives you the advantage of being able to measure the impact and return on everything you try.

Using bricks and mortar as a marketing tool

Being digital-first is slowly starting to change for Huel. They recently launched their first products into grocery stores. The products in these environments are not the core lines (i.e. the powdered meals). Instead, the products they are selling in the supermarkets are ready-to-drink versions of their shakes and also Huel-branded healthy snack bars. Julian has resisted the urge to put the core lines into retail because he believes you need the complete experience with the shaker and t-shirt to get into it properly. Furthermore, you also need to be able to set up a subscription easily. Before you start thinking this is just another DTC brand going mainstream and selling in retail, incremental sales are not Julian's key motivation.

'I would not advise a DTC business to do retail until they have ticked all the other boxes. Retail is a distraction, and you can easily get side-tracked by making retailers happy rather than your end consumers.' Why do it at all, then? 'Two reasons, first there are times when you want a healthy snack when you are out and about, and as well as helping on these occasions which we can't satisfy with our powders, it also extends our reach and builds more brand awareness.'

Retail distribution as a marketing tool is not a new idea, but it's rare to find someone who admits brand awareness is their primary goal. This is the new omnichannel world we live in. Some brands use DTC to build brand awareness and customer connection but still make most of their money in bricks and mortar, and some, like Huel, look at retail to grow awareness more than sales. It is no surprise to see Julian taking an unconventional approach to building new channels. He and his team are true mavericks. Their innovative approach is reflected by the way they operate through to the products they make. For me, they make it work because of their unwavering commitment to incredible customer service, because they deliver a great product experience, and they have products that solve a big problem. Julian was right, even if he is a bit weird, he is not that weird, and there are plenty of similar people who value his approach to health and nutrition. With its unique products, a loyal and growing band of Hueligans and deep international reach, it would seem the sky's the limit for Huel. This really could be the future of food.

LESSONS LEARNT FROM HUEL

1 They found a big problem to be solved and pivoted towards it. The original Bodyhack idea was flawed, but it uncovered an enormous unmet need; how to achieve the optimal balance of nutrients, vitamins and other essential dietary requirements in a quickly prepared and consumed format. Julian would never have found this problem or solution without experimenting with adjacent ideas first.

2 At every step, they made sure the product was fit for DTC. Julian made sure he could justify a high enough price point to cover his distribution costs and create a customer experience good enough to make his customers come back again and again.

3 He made sure his business could prosper and meet his aims, even if it was small. He only needed 1000 customers to make his initial business model work. As well as taking the pressure off, it also meant he did not require huge amounts of capital to get started.

4 The free t-shirts and shakers enabled Huel to build a tribe of proud badge-wearing 'Hueligans'. This on-show advocacy promotes both loyalty with existing customers and increases curiosity and awareness amongst potential new recruits.

5 Being nice and not being a 'dick' promotes a culture of excellent customer service and customer satisfaction. Not only is this a more fun way of doing business, but it's also smart. Happy customers mean lower CAC (customer acquisition costs) and higher LTVs (lifetime value).

6 Don't go into retail until you are ready to. The retail environment is very different from online, and unless you have the resources for it, it can become an unwanted distraction to the rest of the business.

Note

1 The '1000 True Fans Theory' was proposed by *Wired* magazine's Kevin Kelly and states that all a creator needs is 1000 true fans to be successful. The full idea can be found here: kk.org/thetechnium/1000-true-fans/ (archived at https://perma.cc/8LFU-R7P8)

03

Unearthing a huge problem hidden in plain sight

Snag

Whoa, this is going to work a lot better than we had thought.
— BRIE READ, FOUR HOURS AFTER LAUNCHING SNAGTIGHTS.COM

In a world where just about anything you can imagine is available at the click of a button, it is easy to think that all the good ideas have already 'been thought' and all the products we need have already been produced, packaged up, branded and released to the world. If you ever feel frustrated and defeated by the thought that if only you had started to think about setting up a business five years ago rather than now, the story of Snag tights is one for you.

In less than three years, Snag has built a business with revenues over £3 million a month, and customers from around the world, for a single product range that has existed forever and is available in just about any clothing shop, pharmacy and convenience store. What's more, it was all achieved with only £100k of seed investment. How this happened and how quickly Snag has become an enormous success should inspire us all. It is a reminder that there is an infinite number of problems to be solved, that so many needs are left unmet and that the best ideas are often hiding in plain sight.

A quantifiable problem

It all started when Snags founder Brie Read walked down George Street, Edinburgh's main retail thoroughfare, when her tights began to fall down. They did not slip down just by a bit; they worked their way all the way down to below her knees. 'It was really embarrassing and one of those things you take to heart,' explained Brie.

> When I told my friends about it, they all understood the problem only too well. Whether they were short or tall or tiny or big, they all agreed it was impossible to find a pair of tights that fitted properly. It was a crazy idea, how could a product that nearly all women wear be so bad? So, to understand how big the problem was, I set up a Google survey of 3000 women across the UK, and it came back that 90 per cent of women cannot ever find tights which fitted them properly.

Recognizing that you may not be the only one with a problem is one thing but setting up a national survey is not typically how you work out if you are right. That is unless you have a background in data science, which is precisely what Brie had.

Brie was a Computer Science and Psychology graduate, disciplines that have shaped her career in profound ways. As a self-confessed data nerd, Brie first made a name for herself by learning that numbers should drive all product strategy. Her intuitive feel for how numbers should inform marketing decisions bore fruit very early in her career when she was asked to use her numerical skills to become sales and marketing director just a few years into her first job after leaving university. It was a daunting prospect for someone who confessed to knowing very little about marketing at the time. But, while Brie was a novice at marketing, she knew her numbers and turned to the data to seek answers. By employing this approach, she could see things her more traditionally minded predecessors could not. Brie's first act was to remove 90 per cent of their product lines (the company sold educational courses) and remove the discounts from its bestselling products. Most people in the business thought she was insane. Despite the initial shock and cynicism, the results were immediate. The remaining 10 per cent of the lines accounted for nearly all of the company's sales and for Brie it was madness to discount the products with the highest demand. The company went on to sell the same number of courses while at the same time making more than double the profits. Brie continued, 'For me, it was a real wow moment. I realized if you could apply the insights of the numbers, you could become way more efficient. From then on, I was effectively a marketeer, but one with faith that I could solve problems with data.'

Brie went on to serve as marketing director and then CEO for several companies, including Diet Chef and the Post Code Lottery, always focusing on 'what is the data telling us about what our customers want from our products'. Given her success and background in data and computer science, she inevitably ended up in a tech company when she became CEO of Dosadi Ventures. Dosadi Ventures was at the time the UK's largest Facebook advertising agency, helping businesses get the most out of their Facebook adverts.

It was while she was at the social media agency that she had her George Street moment and used her data science background to answer the question, 'is it just me, or is this a really big problem waiting to be solved?' She knew she needed some solid data to answer the question beyond her circle of sympathetic and empathetic friends. Hence the Google survey.

Satisfying the customer need

When the results arrived, it was impossible to interpret the survey data in any other way than, to quote Brie, 'This opportunity is huge, and we would be stupid not to try and fix the problem.' According to Brie, the problem with tights is primarily a legacy issue that's a mix of (1) a commoditized market, (2) that product decisions are made mainly by men (who are not generally the end customer) and (3) because women have become so used to poorly fitting tights they have accepted that this is just the way it is.

Armed with this knowledge, Brie spent a couple of years finding the right manufacturer who understood the issues and agreed to team up to help fix them. It may be easy to think Snag is an overnight success;

however, this underestimates Brie's efforts to get the business in shape before launch. In addition to the challenges of calculating the size of the problem and figuring out how to make a much better product at a competitive price, Brie was also already figuring out her sales and marketing plan. The sales would be made direct to consumer, initially through a simple one-page Shopify site. Critically, she knew she needed margins that would work with 25 per cent of revenue being channelled straight back into marketing the business. 25 per cent of margin straight back into marketing is significantly more than a traditional operating model for a retail brand. However, from a standing start, Brie knew she would have to spend money to generate awareness. Brie also knew how much it costs to advertise on Facebook, and she knew that she needed to have enough cash available for this type of marketing. The majority of DTC businesses know they will need to spend serious amounts of money on promoting their products to attract customers they need to achieve their growth targets. This requirement is why many brands raise large amounts of money from investors to give them money to do this, hoping to reach the scale where the profits will be enough to cover their costs. Brie's alternative strategy was to make sure her profit margins from each sale would be enough to cover her marketing costs from the get-go. This approach meant that she could keep any fundraising to a minimum.

Brie did not completely bootstrap the business. She raised a seed round from her network, conservatively raising about £100k. This money was to pay for the first proper production run to get some inventory into the system. The cash was needed for stock, not to pay for people, product development or advertising. If they could sell the stock, the contribution from sales would pay for these things.

The launch and immediate traction

It was time to go live. There was no grand unveiling or launch party. According to Brie,

> To be honest, I wasn't sure I should do it, but the opportunity was clear, and we had done the work with the manufacturer. We had cobbled

together a website which I had hooked up to a Facebook advertising account. Sitting in Victoria Station late one afternoon waiting for a train, we unceremoniously put the website live. When I checked the numbers that evening, not only were real sales coming in but there were also a lot more of them than we had ever anticipated. I was like, whoa, this is going to work a lot better than we had thought.

The mix of the differentiated products, the marketing messages and the Facebook ads were doing the job of bringing the brand to people's attention. Sales jumped from £15k in the first month to £300k a month in less than a year. In their first full year of trading, they did £2.3 million in sales. And it did not stop there. Second-year sales were £13.3 million, and now, in 2021, in only their third year, they are on track for over £30 million, with revenues now hitting £3 million per month. This sort of growth is atypical. Not even DTC icons like Gymshark have a better growth story in the same time frame.

Having a better product is at the heart of Snag's success, but just as critical has been its ability to find customers and create a lasting connection with the brand. Understanding how to advertise on Facebook and Instagram helps tactically. However, it's in the marketing fundamentals where Snag creates lasting value. To ensure the brand is not seasonal, they change the selection depending on the time of year and website region. For example, they make sure they have thick tights on display in UK winter, with thin and footless versions offered up simultaneously in Australia. In addition, they make sure their models are reflective of the customer mix across their regional websites. For example, they will use completely different models for the same tights in the US, compared to the one used for the UK or Germany. The different looks, sizes, shapes and sexes of their models help their customers relate to the brand and gave them confidence that Snag is a product for them and not for an unattainable aspirational version of themselves. The business is also obsessed with great customer service, ensuring they can give local support in all their markets and always have someone on hand to help with customer issues or questions. Listening to their customers' suggestions resulted in a brand new product, 'Chub Rub' shorts, essentially a pair of tights cut off above the knee, for extra comfort, when you still want to show off your legs. This product was such a hit that they sold their entire summer UK launch stock in less than two weeks when they introduced the line in 2019.

Unsurprisingly for a data devotee, Brie lets the numbers guide her in their most critical strategic decisions. For example, which countries to launch in are driven by the location of website hits and the number of international orders in that region. The size and shape of the models on the website are dependent on the most popular sizes sold. You won't find many size 0 models on the website as the numbers tell them they are not selling products to women of that shape. For this reason, up to 10 per cent of models wearing the tights on the website are male models. The data shows them that up to 10 per cent of their products are bought and worn by men.

The benefits of superior customer service

Brie and her team do a great job of looking after their customers' sizing requirements, customer service returns and championing sustainability (materials, production processes and transport are all made as low impact as possible). All of which build brand loyalty. Doing this is good for business at the best of times. However, it can also make all the difference when tough and unexpected events arrive, particularly ones that threaten to take the whole business down. Brie found out what it means to have a loyal and inventive customer base when the COVID-19 pandemic rapidly put an end to business as normal in March 2020.

The sudden lockdown across the world meant that overnight, over 65 per cent of the Snag business disappeared. Export sales either did not or could not happen, and domestic orders suffered as everyone had other things on their mind rather than buying their next pair of tights for work or a big event. Brie picks up the story:

> When Covid first hit, we were not that worried. We had made a decent amount of money the year before. We used the excess stock we had to

do our bit and donated 24,000 pairs to NHS workers. Our focus was on looking after our people as well as helping wherever else we could. It was only after a month or so into the pandemic that we realized we had a big problem. We had become used to steady growth largely driven by our advertising spend with Facebook. In the months leading up to the lockdown, we had continued to spend heavily on Facebook. It was only when we realized that we still had to pay our bills, but suddenly we had no money coming in to do this, we realized we might not survive. Out of nowhere, we were £800,000 in debt with £600,000 of that owed to Facebook, who had no interest in giving us more time to pay our bills. Our CFO ran the numbers and gave us the news that unless we quickly found some cash, we would be out of business by July.

Most businesses do things like renege on supplier payment agreements, shed staff and put up prices when cash flows dry up. Snag instead used the customer loyalty and goodwill they had built to find a much more elegant solution. The Snag model ensures the products are sold at the lowest price possible all year round, which is why they do not run promotions. However, the cash crunch forced them to change tack. They set up a promotion but one with a twist. Brie explained:

> I thought to myself, yeah, that's it, we are shutting up shop. So in a very Snag way, I went on Instagram and started talking to our customers about what was happening. Not only were they incredibly supportive, but it was they who came up with the idea for this amazing scheme. It was a two for one offer, but they don't get their second pair of tights for another six months. This deal made sense for everyone, the customers get money off, and in addition to some tights now, they get a nice new pair just before Christmas. In return, we get the money for both pairs right away. The idea came together on Sunday, we launched it on Monday, and by Friday, we had £1.25M in the bank. It was insane.

The business got through that crisis and has since started to grow at pace again. Snag is an organization that continues to be guided by the numbers, with each web visit, purchase and customer interaction showing them the way. Being a skilled data scientist and using the numbers to give her team the confidence to try things out is paying off for Brie. She did, however, offer me one last bit of advice, 'You know, having [numerical] skill is useful, but you also need to be thinking about the data points as actual people, not just clicks or numbers.' If a data scientist can remember that, there can be no excuse for the rest of us.

LESSONS FROM SNAG

1 Brie used her personal day to day experiences to uncover a vast problem (poorly fitting tights) that was not currently being addressed. She also made sure she did some rigorous market research to determine if it was only her or a much bigger issue.

2 Brie learned an early lesson that her weaknesses in one area (traditional marketing expertise) could be overcome by using her strength in another (in her case, data science). Tackling a problem with a different approach can often uncover solutions that would otherwise be missed.

3 Let data drive your strategy. Brie and the team use data to better understand their customers' needs and then make products that can meet that requirement. They use the data to make sure they know who their customers are and make sure their marketing resonates. They also use website and sales data to tell them which regions to tackle next.

4 When funding the business, Brie made sure her margins could cover the marketing costs the brand would need. She did not rely on raising enormous amounts of investment and hoping she could spend it on marketing and scale her way to profitability.

5 Snag used social media to have very open communication channels with their customers. This is not only great customer service but also builds lasting connections. In regular times this a great way to build the brand and understand the needs, wants and desires of their customers, e.g. Chub Rub shorts. It was also critical when they needed to act quickly and could crowdsource support and ideas from their customer base. Their ongoing investment into customer relationships saved the day when the COVID-19 pandemic threatened to bankrupt the business.

6 While data drives decisions, Brie was keen to remind us all that every data point results from the actions and behaviours of a real human being. So you have to look beyond the clicks and numbers to understand who your customer really is and to make sure you are doing right by them.

04

Measuring satisfaction
and why it matters

Bloom & Wild

In the early 2000s, the management consultancy company Bain & Co. came up with a scientific method of measuring customer satisfaction. They called it net promoter score or NPS.

The NPS method works like this: you ask a set of customers to score their satisfaction out of 10, and depending on the result, they split the scores into three groups: promoters, detractors and passives. Promoters are those who love and appreciate what you do. They are the ones most likely to buy your products regularly and crucially are also likely to spread the word telling their friends, colleagues and family. On the other hand, detractors are those who do not like your products or your service. Assuming they have a choice, they would not be a customer and would also actively dissuade others from trying you out. That leaves passives who likely view your product or service as okay but lack any enthusiasm, which means that they would unlikely give you another thought, whether that be positive or negative. Passives neither help nor hinder your cause and, therefore, can be ignored according to the NPS methodology. In the NPS method, scores of 9 and 10 are classed as promoters, scores of 6 and under are detractors, and anything else is deemed passive.

The calculation for your NPS is the percentage of promoters minus the percentage of detractors. The maximum score is 1 (or 100%), and a minimum of –1 (or –100%). Any score close to or below 0 indicates low satisfaction levels. For example, consider if 11 people are asked to score how much they are likely to recommend a new type of yoghurt. Two score 9, two score 8, three score 7, three score 5 and 1 scores 2. To calculate NPS using these results, the calculation would be:

Percentage of promoters – percentage of detractors = (2/11)–(4/11) = (18%)–(36%) = –18%. Or –0.18.

In this example, even though more than half of the respondents scored over 7, the number of passives (people who don't care very much) and the number of detractors (people who will tell others about their dissatisfaction) results in a negative score, indicating the product may struggle. Thus, NPS is a way to determine the great from the merely good, the good from the okay and the okay from the bad. The theory is that wherever choice is abundant, a high NPS score signals the best chance of acquiring new customers.

NPS is not perfect and does not apply in every situation; however, the method has been widely adopted. None more so than at Bain & Co., where they've used it across multiple industries and have shown that a high NPS directly correlates with higher revenue growth.[1]

Bain and Co. is also where Aron Gelbard went to work once he completed his Harvard MBA. Aron has the kind of academic background that makes him very employable among the top consultancy firms. However, what made Aron different from most of his peers was a combination of an entrepreneurial heritage and a burning desire to make other people happy.

Uncovering an industry ready for disruption

So when, a couple of years into his stint with Bain, Aron discovered a massive industry with a consistently low level of customer satisfaction (measured by NPS, of course), he had found what he was looking for. The industry in question was Flowers and Floristry. The market was huge, but there was dissatisfaction across multiple considerations: poor selection, short shelf life, delivery issues and regularly substituted products, to name a few. The industry was trying to correct these issues, but this resulted in higher costs, more waste and more complexity. It was these problems causing the poor NPS scores when measured by management consultants.

Low NPS scores bother Aron. Trying to improve things appeals to his intellectual problem-solving nature, but it also genuinely bugs him that people are unhappy and annoyed by doing something that should bring joy (like buying flowers).

Aron had been waiting for a chance like this. Here was an industry that was failing its customers and therefore was ripe for a new way of doing things. Even so, it required a good deal of bravery to leave his well-paid consultancy job. Ultimately, it was his family background in entrepreneurship that gave him the final push. For Aron, now was the chance to follow in the footsteps of his two grandfathers and his father, who had each previously set up their own very successful businesses. One side of the family were chocolate producers and the other finding their niche in plastic recycling.

More choice, better service, superior value

I am guessing I am like most in that I have often purchased flowers but had never considered the inner workings of growers, flower distribution and the difficulties faced by a modern florist. Traditionally, florists have been the place to go for a bunch of flowers either as a gift or to brighten up your home. There is always something incredibly wholesome about seeing the bunches of flowers lovingly arranged in the shop window. Florists also provide a burst of colour and appealing aromas to your average high street. Alas, high-street florists have been on the decline for decades. I have certainly noticed this sad trend but have never really questioned why. Chatting with Aron helped me understand the challenges.

Aron explained:

> the industry had been running this relay model, which relied on lots
> of smaller florists that had to rely on these long supply chains and

were also expected to stock hundreds of types of flowers. So, as well as resulting in poor product quality, flowers had also become very expensive due to the middlemen needed to put the products and customers together.

Price was the main reason people stopped buying flowers from their local florist and instead started picking them up from the supermarket. At the supermarket, costs may have been lower, but selection and quality were still a problem. Supermarkets are also a very transactional way to buy flowers. It is harder to cherish a bunch of flowers when they lay in your basket next to a tin of beans and a packet of wet wipes.

With traditional florists struggling to compete with the supermarkets and the supermarket (or garage forecourt) experience taking the love out of buying flowers, it left a real consumer problem waiting to be solved. So it was in 2013, Aron left his consultancy job and co-founded Bloom & Wild, a flower company that would use technology to solve the problems inherent in the traditional florist system.

DTC consumer businesses are built on the promise of cutting out the long and expensive supply chains associated with traditional retail models. These long supply chains are due to the complex cast of characters involved to get a product onto a retailer shelf. This ensemble includes a retail buyer who decides which products to stock and how much they will sell for, a distributor who will purchase products from the supplier and the supplier who will specify to a manufacturer what to make and when to make it. What's more in some markets, there is also the need for importers, brokers and merchandizers to join the chain to manoeuvre a product from the point of manufacture into the hands of the end consumer. Lengthy and complicated supply chains have so many touchpoints and resource requirements that it is inevitable that costs soon rack up.

Connecting the manufacturer with the end consumer without the need for a long and expensive supply chain is the promise that DTC brands have always highlighted as their primary advantage. They also do not have to fear a supermarket buyer not taking a risk on stocking a new product or brand, limiting choice. Provided brands can drive awareness, DTC promises more choice, better service and superior value.

Flowers through your letterbox

Creating a distribution advantage was a crucial challenge for Bloom and Wild. However, Aron and his team discovered it was not easy to get flowers safely from the grower to the end customer. Traditionally, bouquets were big, bulky and delicate. Along with careful handling required, from the point, they were arranged into each bunch, which meant they had to be hand-delivered directly to the recipient, preferably upright and in water.

Bloom and Wild could not be successful until they found a way to get their flowers from A to B more robustly. Aron explained the solution:

> The perception was that flowers always needed to be kept upright and hydrated, but we learned the flowers were not hydrated further back in the supply chain. Once we had learnt this, we started to question whether having flowers in water was due to customer expectation versus what actually needs to happen.

Aron worked out you could deliver non-hydrated flowers that were still in bud (before the petals open), and they'd still have a long shelf life. Shipping flowers around, out of water, was how things happened before they reached the retailer. But could it work for DTC? The other advantage of moving flowers without them being upright and in water was that they could be packed into a cardboard box. Furthermore, as flowers are generally long and thin, you can put them in a long thin box. Putting this all together, Bloom & Wild created the letterbox bouquet. A bunch of flowers delivered in a box that could be posted through the door.

This idea was novel, and anything new carries the risk that it would not be liked. Indeed Aron initially feared that customers would not adopt the idea. He needn't have worried. 'It was a radical idea, and we were fortunate that it was even more popular than we expected.' With the flowers being able to be put through the letterbox, you no longer needed to worry about the recipient being there to receive the flowers when they were delivered. This method also made arranging the flowers yourself an easy and satisfying thing to do. Each bouquet includes a style guide with hints and tips about arranging and caring for your bouquet. A small packet of flower food is also added for extra longevity.

According to Aron, it was the introduction of the letterbox flower concept that made the business. He explained, 'We were very differentiated, and the novelty appealed to people. We also really cared about the things that our customers desired, which generated good review scores and advocacy.' The demand and the positive feedback were the fuel that attracted both customers and investors. Today, the business has over 400 employees and more than 4 million customers, to whom they send millions of bouquets each year.

Overall, the business has been an enormous success and has transformed the experience of buying and receiving flowers. However, not all the initial assumptions Aron and his team made proved to be correct. Initially, they thought they would be a flower subscription business when, in fact, the core customer need was gifting. The technology requirements also turned out to be way more significant and complex than initially imagined.

The importance of managing your technology

Surprisingly for a technology business, initially, it was the tech and engineering that proved the biggest struggle. 'The cost of building the technology needed was much higher than expected. We tried to outsource a lot of the tech build, but this turned out to be expensive and inefficient. In the end, we raised some more cash and invested in an in-house team,' explained Aron. This investment has since paid back, and Bloom & Wild has grown from a relatively green business when it came to technology to one recognized as an expert in e-commerce. They even have a 'tech blog' on their website, full of thought pieces, experiences, and tips and tricks from their engineering team. As well as helping with knowledge and ideas internally, the tech blog has become a resource for insight and inspiration for the whole DTC community.

More thoughtful marketing

When Bloom & Wild discovered that the primary demand from their customers was not regular subscriptions but gifting, it meant a change in their marketing strategy. If not subscription, they had to look to other ways to generate repeat purchases. The first trick was to deliver high customer satisfaction; without this, no amount of marketing would motivate customers to buy again. Then to create repeat sales, Bloom & Wild would rely heavily on emailing their customers. The purpose of these emails is primarily to act as a prompt and remind their customers how lovely it is to receive a bunch of flowers as a gift. Once you sign up for an account, there are also handy tools on the website for setting reminders for birthdays and anniversaries. From my desk, at least, receiving an email prompt and a simple method to buy my wife flowers a few days before her birthday, is the sort of email that provides a lot of value.

Of course, they also send out more emails for collective occasions like Mother's Day. While this is a very useful nudge to many customers, mentions of specific celebrations can also pose an unwanted and sometimes painful reminder to others. This undesirable consequence of email marketing led to a new initiative, pioneered by Bloom & Wild, called the 'Thoughtful Marketing Movement'. The general idea is to give your customers the ability to easily opt out of emails tailored for events such as Mother's Day or Father's Day and to do so forever.

It was not an easy thing for their engineering team to deliver, and it certainly makes it harder to manage all of the contact lists a company like Bloom and Wild needs to have to communicate with their customers. However, their customers overwhelmingly appreciated the concept and the ability to personalize their needs. The feedback was so positive and heartfelt, Bloom & Wild were inspired to share their experience and process with other brands and encouraged them to do the same with their email lists. In less than a year, other UK brands and organizations, including Paperchase, *The Telegraph*, Marie Curie, The Body Shop, Treatwell and many more, were active participants in the movement. The idea has also spread to the United States, where Etsy, Pandora and Away allow you to permanently 'opt out' of prompts for specific occasions.

The Thoughtful Marketing Movement, the tech blog and the core activity of great flowers through the letterbox exemplify a tireless desire to make people that bit happier than before they had discovered Bloom & Wild.

NPS is maybe just a number, but for Aron and his team, it measures happiness. When you have a deep-rooted desire to please people and fix problems, it is a number that motivates. The consultants at Bain & Co. will also remind us that getting NPS right is also good for business. Whatever the motivation, the benefit for Bloom & Wild is over 4 million happy customers. Everyone should be satisfied with that.

LESSONS FROM BLOOM & WILD

1   Find a product or industry with low levels of customer satisfaction and work out how you can fix the problem. Just as Snag did for tights, Bloom & Wild found a way to solve the pain points of buying flowers.

2   Find a quantifiable method to measure satisfaction. Aron is a big advocate of NPS, but it is not the only way to measure delight. Customer surveys, reviews, click rates and interviews can all measure satisfaction so long as the data is accessible and there is a measurable way to assess the results.

3   The critical innovation of the letterbox bouquet was realized by looking at what happened further back in the supply chain and finding a way to adapt those processes to give the consumer a better experience. It's always a risk to defy convention, but if you think there is a better way to meet your customers' needs, it may be worth a try.

4   DTC brands use technology to better connect with and serve their customers. This means you need to get your technical capability right. At

first, Bloom & Wild struggled as they outsourced their engineering and underestimated what it would take to build the product they needed. However, once they realized they needed to invest more and bring it in-house, not only did it allow them to get things under control, they found it easier to offer additional features and services.

5 By focusing on customer satisfaction, they discovered their emails were causing pain to specific subsections of their customer base. Prompts to buy flowers on Mother's Day or Father's Day were not what some customers wanted to receive. Allowing customers to opt out of specific email campaigns without unsubscribing from everything fixed this problem and further increased appreciation for the company's service. This idea has been so well received that it has spread and has become a movement adopted by DTC businesses worldwide.

Note

1 Source: www.bain.com/consulting-services/customer-strategy-and-marketing/customer-loyalty/ (archived at https://perma.cc/QV8T-E8SW)

05

Moving with the times and the art of resilience

Cornerstone

The pace of change

One of the problems with writing this book is how quickly the DTC landscape is changing. Even during the writing of this book, I have had to work hard to make sure what you read is still relevant and actionable by the time it reaches your bookshelf. My job has been to identify the signal from the noise and work out what qualities will give you the best chance of success, whether you started your business in 2012 or 2022 and beyond. To better understand the changes over the last decade, it was helpful to talk to someone who has successfully navigated their way through them.

It seems generous to call someone in their early thirties an industry veteran; however, given everything he has achieved and worked through, Cornerstone founder and CEO Oliver Bridge has the tenure and the talent to qualify. Cornerstone, founded in 2014, was initially the UK's answer to Dollar Shave Club (launched in the United States the previous year), selling quality razor blades on subscription. Since then, both Cornerstone and the DTC landscape have changed dramatically. Competition, marketing costs, technology, the attitude of investors and consumer expectations have all evolved. For Cornerstone to have succeeded during this time, they have had to develop at the same pace and course-correct at the right time.

Early entrepreneurial endeavours

Like many of the founders I have interviewed for this project, Oliver has been setting up businesses for as long as he can remember. It started with the typical kid's lemonade stand set-up and then escalated from there. First up was a self-published magazine, *Star Best*, printed on his dad's photocopier. *Star Best*'s success ultimately depended on the kindness of Oliver's neighbours, with Oliver's local sweet shop also benefiting from their generosity. When Oliver was a little older, next came a mobile disco to hire and finally, at the age of 15, a bona fide business selling shoes online. The business was called Biggerfeet.com and was an e-commerce business sourcing shoes for people with larger than average feet, a demographic that included Oliver. He explained:

> Buying shoes was a problem, so I decided to do something about it. This was before shoes were widely available on the web. Even Amazon was still mainly books and CDs at the time. I went to a few trade shows, and even now, I am not sure how, but I managed to convince some shoe suppliers to set me up as a wholesale customer and a business was born. I went to school in the day, did my homework and then spent each evening processing orders, sorting stock and ordering more inventory. We were quite successful, and I went from handing out flyers in the local village to being on the front cover of the local newspaper and eventually being featured on CNN.

Running a successful business part-time is hard, especially so when you are still at school. When Oliver's end-of-school exams loomed, his usually encouraging parents pushed Oliver to spend less time on the business and more on his education. It was time to knuckle down to the books and move on. However, that was not the end of Biggerfeet.com as Oliver had already found a buyer for it – his younger brother, who continued to run it for several years while Oliver went off to university. The business eventually ceased operations when Amazon expanded beyond books and music, leaving Biggerfeet.com unable to compete with an internet full of more developed e-commerce websites offering prices lower than the Bridges could buy wholesale.

Although he went to university with the aspiration of getting into investment banking, it had become reasonably predictable that Oliver was never going to follow a traditional career path. Even while studying for his degree, Oliver continued to tinker with entrepreneurial ideas. While at university and following a stint working for a charity, he set up Genderchecker.com. At the charity, his job was to call lots of London councils. Due to the diversity in the cosmopolitan city, he found the people he had to talk to did not usually have traditional Anglo-Saxon names but names deriving from every corner of the planet. He often felt embarrassed that he did not know how to properly address them as he had no idea whether the name on his call sheet was male or female. After first seeking out a database to help and finding out it did not exist, he decided to create his own. Motivated by his awkward personal experiences, he created Genderchecker.com, an online resource to double-check the likely gender of any name. Genderchecker.com would grow to a database of over 102,000 names, with customers benefiting from the list, including the UN, the Red Cross and Microsoft. Oliver still owns the business, and it still brings in steady monthly revenues.

From VC to founder

With his drive for creating businesses, it was somewhat of a surprise to learn that upon graduating, he became a full-time employee. First for an innovation consultancy then working for a venture capital fund investing in consumer brands. Being on the payroll would not last, especially as these jobs gave him first-hand experience of consumer brands, new technology and finance, the exact skills you need to run a DTC business. However, Oliver first needed to figure out what his business should be.

Again, it was a personal problem that provided the answer. When Oliver was 15, he had trouble buying shoes and saw the opportunity to solve that problem for himself and others. Ten years later, he had the same insight with another product he needed but could not easily get. It was 2013, and the 25-year-old Oliver's issue was that he had sensitive skin. All the big branded razors and shaving creams were leaving his skin raw after his daily shave.

Further inspiration came from the United States, where a new business called Dollar Shave Club had just launched. His own painful shaving experience and the success of Dollar Shave Club convinced Oliver that a UK based DTC razor blade business was what he should do next. 'No one was doing it here, so I am going to do it in Europe in a really classy way.'

Oliver was keen to stress while Cornerstone was about razors through the post, the focus was much more about product quality and helping men with sensitive skin than a rock bottom price. So it was a bonus when he realized that he could compete on both price and quality by removing the wholesalers and retailers from the value chain.

Finding suppliers and building a plan from the kitchen table

With the idea in place, Oliver got to work with formulating a business plan and pulling together everything he would need to launch the business. The first job was to find a razor supplier. There are not many manufacturers around for razor blades, and doing it himself was out of his reach due to existing patents and high tooling costs. Fortunately, after a search, Oliver found a particular German manufacturer who could make the right product at the right price. The only problem was minimum order quantities.

Oliver takes up the story:

> I was sitting around my kitchen table, in my London flat, and I phoned up the factory and said I would like to place an order for 5000 razor blades. The sales manager said you must be joking; the minimum order quality is 1 million! I thought this could be game over. Then I asked him how about if I got to his office at 9 am the following morning and gave him €5000 in cash? His response was something like if you are crazy enough to do that, he would see what he could do.

Challenge accepted. Oliver got his euros together, roped in his stepfather and critically his stepfather's car. That same afternoon they headed off to the Eurotunnel and drove through the night across France into Germany. As promised, Oliver was sitting in the factory's reception at 8.45 am, asking to see the sales manager. With a glint in his eye, Oliver recalled:

> When he saw me sitting there, he just doubled over in laughter, gave me a pat on the back, took the cash, wrote out the invoice and got two pallets of razors forked around to the car, which my stepfather and I loaded into the boot and back seat. The rapport and relationship had been established, and we had our launch stock.

With the razors secured, Oliver set about raising money to pay for the branded Cornerstone handles and the skincare products that would complete the kits. He eventually raised £150,000 from angel investors, which also gave him the money he needed to create the brand and build the website.

The business plan, the funding and the work to launch the business was all done while Oliver was still holding down his day job. Whenever he found time at the weekends and before and after work, he built his new business from his kitchen table. Oliver admitted that one of his proudest achievements was the astonishment of his bosses at the VC fund when he revealed he was quitting his job to pursue this new venture. His old bosses could not believe how much planning and preparation he had already done while still doing everything that was expected of him in his day job. They had no idea they were about to lose a star employee. A week after quitting his job, still sitting at his kitchen table, Cornerstone was launched.

Experiments in customer acquisition

After all the set-up costs, including inventory, branding and the website, Oliver had about £100,000 left to prove he could generate enough sales to show his plan could work. With limited customer acquisition experience, Oliver experimented digitally with social and paid-for channels like Facebook, Google and Twitter. He also tried handing out fliers and encouraging everyone he knew to try the product. With about half the marketing pot spent on testing and not getting very far, Oliver started to wonder whether he would soon be asking for his old job back. Eventually, they found their breakthrough. They put a post on Reddit, entitled 'Do you enjoy shaving?'

> We asked how many people had a problem with their shave and skin, and we introduced the brand. The post started trending, and we soon had 1000 customers. These 1000 customers enabled us to do some Facebook ads using the look-alike function, and we were on a roll. 1000 customers turned into 5000 customers over the next 12 weeks.

One of the things they discovered from their first few thousand customers and then the ones that followed via the look-alike function was that the brand was not being picked up by the demographic they had initially assumed. The initial target group was 25- to 35-year-old city-dwelling millennials. Instead, the data told them that most of their customers were suburban 30- to 50-year-old family men. They also found that around 75 per cent of their customers came to the brand primarily because they had sensitive skin, with the other 25 per cent for the experience and convenience. This allowed them to make their targeting and marketing messages even more effective.

Free cash

The big difference between a DTC business in 2014 and in 2022 is how much money you need to spend to bring in a new customer. Back in 2014, so long as you had a good product, had worked out whom to target and had moderate to no competition, your acquisition costs would be small. If you were lucky, as most first movers at this time were, your acquisition costs would be lower than profits from each customer you convert. In this scenario, the more money you spend on marketing and customer acquisition, the bigger and more profitable your business will become. Oliver explained the situation back then as 'Once we had worked out who our customers were, it was like a free cash flow cycle and we just could not get enough money to feed the system. You wanted to mortgage your house and spend the money on Facebook. It was the golden age and so began our meteoric rise.'

Investors agreed that risks were low and rewards were high. Within 24 months, Cornerstone had raised nearly £8 million, including £1 million from crowdfunding from their customer base. While it was not the biggest of their rounds, it was the crowdfunding that Oliver particularly liked. By crowdfunding, they created an investor community of brand advocates who would actively promote the brand. It also gave the company hundreds of engaged investors to call on for advice and feedback on new products and marketing ideas.

The arrival of better-funded competition

Unfortunately for Oliver and his investors, the UK male grooming marketplace was about to become a lot more competitive. In the previous few years, Cornerstone had already seen off lots of lower price competitors who may have had an attractive price but did not have comparable product quality nor could offer the same level of customer service. Unlike Cornerstone, these differences meant that they could not build a loyal customer base and ultimately could not grow at the same rate. Cornerstone, however, faced a much beefier challenge as the well-funded US DTC razor companies, Dollar Shave Club and, in particular, Harry's chose to expand into the UK.

The arrival of Harry's transformed the landscape dramatically for Cornerstone. The big difference between Cornerstone and Harry's and the other DTC brands from the United States was the funding and scale of these businesses. Oliver explained that these US brands had managed to raise hundreds of millions of dollars, putting them in a different league to Cornerstone and other European counterparts. For example, Harry's does not have to worry about being let down by their razor supplier. As part of their launch strategy, they bought a German razor factory for a reported €100 million. In addition to their manufacturing advantages, Harry's scale and buying power also enables them to do more marketing than everyone else. Furthermore, they had resources and margins to expand beyond DTC into traditional retail. Harry's products can now be found on the UK high street in key grocery and pharmacy chains like Boots, Superdrug and Sainsbury's. They also have a UK office to manage and develop their retail base. Oliver admits Cornerstone just does not have the resources or skills to work with these retailers.

Harry's and Dollar Shave Club have also made a big dent in the online marketplace in the UK. Oliver explains:

> This is not only a problem in terms of them having more marketing spend but also because it reduces the total accessible market (TAM) for us. Our initial thinking was that the men's grooming industry was so big that even if there was more competition, there was still plenty of the market to go around. The problem we have is that while the total shaving market is huge, in hindsight, it turns out that the actual market for men who are willing to buy their shaving equipment online is a lot, lot smaller. This means that when someone like Harry's comes into the market, they can quickly erode our market share.

Even with online demand increasing following the changes in shopping habits due to the COVID-19 lockdowns, the SAM (Serviceable Available Market – the total market you can serve given your chosen route to market and geographical reach) for most categories remains a lot smaller than the total market size when retail sales are included.

As explained earlier in this book, the other impact of competition is that it pushes up customer acquisition costs as the price of digital advertising increases. So by the end of the last decade, the 'Golden Age' was over. The competition had become intense, reducing the number of available customers, and the cost of acquiring these customers had increased significantly.

A new strategy

So, where does this leave Cornerstone? First, they have expanded their range and their remit. 'We have adapted pretty well and have moved the business into more products, still with the focus on what a modern man might have in his bathroom cabinet.' These products include ones that suit a discreet online service, including hair loss ointments, erectile dysfunction products, condoms and weight loss treatment. In addition, moisturiser, toothpaste, deodorant and shampoos are now also available. 'Essentially, we want to be a concierge for the modern man. This is why we have added the new products into our portfolio. The requirement to make these changes beyond shaving has given the business a new lease of life,' explained Oliver.

Introducing these new products also continued to build the trust and loyalty Cornerstone has with its customers. Oliver told me why.

> What has reassured me most is that many of our customers have never bought any Viagra-type products or the hair-loss treatment before. We are the first company they have trusted with these sorts of products. I am proud we have been able to build that level of trust into the brand. We did this first through the quality and service of our razors business, and now we are bringing that same level of care and expertise into these new products.

This level of trust has built up over years and years of work. Oliver's take was:

> Our focus has been on quality, good service and using feedback to make the products better. This has resulted in a loyal base of customers who trust us when we bring in new products. We are also fortunate that we can ask for feedback from our existing customers and crowd investors when we are thinking about introducing a new product.

As well as diversifying their product range, the other thing which Cornerstone has done to counter the impact of this new competition is to try not to compete. 'If we tried to compete directly with these businesses who have millions of dollars at their disposal, we would quickly punch ourselves out. Our expectations are more modest, and our focus is on profitable growth, not growth at all costs.'

Better marketing, better products and better service

As well as introducing more products the business has become more efficient with their marketing. They have learnt that they need to make sure they continue to get their targeting right.

> For example, we have never done Groupon. While we could convert a lot of new customers that way, we know they are a lot less likely to stick around. We stick to the high-quality channels with the higher-quality demographics. With Groupon, it may cost us only £1 to acquire a customer, but we know if we spend £10 elsewhere, it will still return a better profit.

These longer-term profits come from retaining a high lifetime value (LTV) from each customer. I asked Oliver about his retention strategy.

> First of all, it's about having a good quality product. There were many lowpricerazor.com type businesses in Europe who launched shortly after us, and we are one of the last ones standing. We have continued to improve our products and service. For example, over the years, we have upgraded suppliers, improved our packaging, added customer tracking to our deliveries, got better with our emails, added personalization like customizable razor blade handles and, above all, continued to improve our customer service capabilities.

Customer service, along with marketing and technology, is one of the critical parts of a DTC business. For that reason, Oliver advocates that you should always keep it in-house. 'It's our internal flywheel; by keeping customer service in-house, we get the feedback to make our products better, make our marketing better and make the technology experience better.'

What to do when subscription becomes less convenient

One other fundamental change has been to alter their approach to their subscription model. From the outset, the requirements and preferences for how often their customers changed their razors varied significantly from one person to the next. This variability always made trying to calculate what the frequency of deliveries should be for any single customer nearly impossible. The solution was to allow customers to work out what they needed and select their frequency for themselves. On top of this, the technology and user experience is designed to make it as simple to pause, snooze and amend subscriptions.

As part of the recent changes, they now have a hybrid model where customers can also place one-off orders in addition to subscribing to products. Oliver explains why this change is also customer-centric:

> We have always liked the subscription model and the membership feeling it gives our customers. Primarily our subscription service has always been about ease and convenience. However, services like Amazon Prime have made subscriptions less important as you can now get a delivery the same day or the next day, which has forced us to adapt. Now shopping using a service like Amazon Prime is so easy having a subscription set up has almost become more inconvenient.

Interestingly, despite their ubiquity and convenient service, you will no longer find Cornerstone products on Amazon. Their absence is because as the brand dabbled with Amazon over the years, they found that Amazon sales cannibalized sales from their website and broke the direct customer link. What's more, the category is now so competitive that the cost of marketing on the platform far outweighs any profits they make from each sale.

Balancing growth and profitability

The last significant change to the business over the last few years is developing a much more disciplined approach towards profit. In the early years, supported by their investors, all the profits and more were ploughed back into the business to grow their customer base. However, as acquisition costs continue to grow, that approach is no longer sustainable. The focus has changed from growth at all costs to a sustainable operating model. Growth is still a critical ambition but is now also balanced against being able to make money without the need for new rounds of investment. An example of the steps to achieve this was reducing the Cornerstone team size from 20-plus employees to 10 or so key individuals. The changing operating environment and a focus on profit seem to suit Oliver. They have forced the business to grow in different directions, all the while maintaining the high standards and levels of trust they established from the very start. In that regard, they have not changed at all.

LESSONS FROM CORNERSTONE

1   Oliver worked on the Cornerstone plan from his kitchen table while still holding down his day job. This approach reduced his risk by making sure his business plan was sound and could attract investors before taking himself off the payroll.

2   The obstacle of high minimum order quantities was no match for Oliver's hustle and ingenuity when he drove across to Germany with an envelope full of cash. Not only did he get the stock, but he also built some early rapport with his supplier.

3   The Cornerstone brand focused on quality and trust. This single-mindedness meant that while there were other potentially cheaper online offers around, Cornerstone customers became loyal. If a cheaper product does not meet a fundamental consumer need (e.g. give you a clean, comfortable shave when you have sensitive skin) or does not arrive on time, customers will ultimately choose quality and service over price.

4   When Harry's entered the market, Cornerstone chose not to compete directly head to head with a vastly better-funded business. Instead, they added new products to their range and changed their positioning. They also avoided the temptation to follow Harry's into retail as they knew they did not have the skills or resources to compete with them and the other traditional shaving giants.

5   They have a customer-first approach. One example of this is keeping customer service in-house. Doing this gives their customers the best possible experience. It also produces instant and consistent feedback to help them improve products, marketing and technology. Another example of better serving their customers is moving away from their subscription-only model to a hybrid offer. They have done this as they understand that subscriptions can sometimes be more inconvenient and hassle than ordering products every time due to new rapid delivery services.

6 To survive, in the long term, they have found a way to balance growth
   and profit. Quick-growth models now often need significant funding.
   Rather than returning to investors, the business is finding ways to grow
   within its means. This balanced approach means smarter use of
   resources and ensuring maximum returns from its marketing efforts.

06

Why bigger is not always better

Sugru

Throughout this book you will find the common theme of building a community as soon as possible, launching your brand on DTC, gaining traction to expand into retail, wholesale and if you can launch internationally. While many brands have enjoyed significant success following this process, it is not applicable or suitable for all brands. Getting your growth strategy wrong can be costly, if not fatal. I was lucky to find a founder who learnt this lesson the hard way and was happy to share their experience.

'Starting small is definitely a good way to go, and as you grow, you need to keep the stakes as low as possible. High costs and investment meant the stakes got very high for us. If you can keep the costs low, the more freedom you will have,' was the refreshing advice Sugru inventor and founder Jane Ní Dhulchaointigh gave to me at the end of our interview.

How big should your DTC brand be?

Ambition is an essential part of business building. Scaling a successful startup is almost impossible without having a grand mission and stretching targets. The stories we are told also influence our definition of what having a successful business looks like. There is an infinite supply of how little ideas and insights quickly scale into companies worth multiple millions. And yes, I am aware that by writing this book, I am adding to the pile. The general narrative is that success is growing rapidly, and you have not really made it until you are big. A get big fast strategy is one way of doing business and is great when it works. However, this strategy can also blow you way off your course if you are not careful with your resources and the cards you are dealt do not fall your way. Sugru is an example of a DTC company that started small, found success and then suffered some nasty growing pains.

Like most of the brands in this book, Sugru is a company that probably would not have happened if it was not for a DTC platform. It is also a company that almost crashed because it tried to be more than a DTC brand and found that life beyond the internet was more demanding than anticipated. Going multichannel is an important strategic choice for a DTC brand. And before making the leap it is essential to weigh the costs and benefits, and the risks and rewards.

What is Sugru?

Sugru has long been one of my favourite DTC brands. They have a wonderfully innovative, useful product and have built an inclusive and helpful community. I have used their products, bought them as gifts and often nudged my friends to check them out. When I was trying to work out how to make Peppersmith better at DTC, it was Sugru that I held up as a brilliant example of what makes a great DTC brand. Beyond their products, they had an attractive website, active social channels, informative and funny videos, exemplary customer service, and they were one of the earliest and best examples of a community-driven product. With this history, I was even more excited and starstruck to meet with Jane and hear her story than many of the more famous brands and founders in this book.

If you have yet to discover the joys of Sugru, 'what is it?' is a great question. The easiest way to describe it is 'mouldable glue' or, as Jane called it in the early days, 'Space-aged Rubber'. Sugru is a flexible, silicone, rubberlike material that you can mould and shape like play-dough. In addition to being extremely mouldable, once it is out of the packet, it starts to react with the environment and within 24 hours is transformed into a solid, strong, flexible, waterproof material. 'What is the use of that?' is an even better follow-up question.

Beginnings

Other than its unique physical properties, the invention is fascinating because it was not a bunch of white-coated chemical engineers who came up with it. It was the result of an art project on a Master's in Design Degree at the RCA (London's Royal College of Art).

Jane's creative odyssey begins back in rural Ireland, where she was brought up on a farm and taught to fix and make rather than to throw and buy. Jane remembered her childhood as, 'Sundays wouldn't be Sundays without mending clothes. I learnt to sew, embroider and was soon customizing my own clothes and jeans. I was also required to observe and then help my dad fix tractors, fences, walls, gates.' As a result, Jane's upbringing was both creative and practical.

Growing up, this was normal, but as a fine art student in London in the early 2000s, she found she was experiencing a clash of cultures. Surrounded by the talent at the RCA, there was plenty of creativity, but to Jane, it mainly seemed like art was being created just for art's sake, which did not sit well with her more practical and resourceful nature. It was only when challenged to be more experimental and design something useful that she found her groove. 'Happy play' was how Jane described this time. One of the things she started to play with was a mouldable silicone that was fun to sculpt and also set hard overnight. But was it useful? The utility was a problem, admitted Jane.

> At the start, there was no single application for what I had created. Other than using it for sculpting, I could not think of any single thing that would be useful for the material, but then I was using the leftovers to fix all sorts of things around the house. It was my now-husband, then-boyfriend, James, who was watching me do this, who first had the

vision of every granny, kid or whoever using this stuff to adapt, improve and mend things like I was doing. I was like, yes, that is just brilliant and set off on a mission to get this product into everyone's kitchen drawer.

Years of product development

Jane's invention drew some nice attention, and she was able to show off a prototype at the prestigious RCA end-of-year summer exhibition. As a result, the product was featured in the British Airways magazine and attracted many inquiries and offers to help. One of those interested was seasoned entrepreneur Roger Ashby. With Ashby's backing, support and encouragement, Jane decided to pursue the idea of bringing her mouldable silicone to market. Initially, the plan was to develop the product, which they would then license to other manufacturers. Easier said than done.

First, Jane had to get the product right. It took an eye-watering six years working on the material to make it practically usable. With some business grants and investment, Jane managed to recruit some expert material scientists to help her develop and refine the product. When I asked how and why she kept going over those long pre-revenue years, she responded that she was used to being a poor student, so used to not having any money. Besides, she was convinced that this thing really could be unique, so she just kept going.

With years of hard work and support from some of the world's best silicone experts, they finally had a product that they were confident would work. However, it was then that they discovered a flaw in their sales strategy. Jane's mouldable glue was so innovative that those companies she thought might like to license and commercialize it turned her down. It was just too radical, and they could not see how it would fit in with their current product mix.

Launching small

With no prospect of licensing, Jane takes up the story:

> I had this vision of this product being in everyone's kitchen drawer.
> However, none of the manufacturers out there saw the opportunity.
> We were also pre-revenue, so raising any more cash was incredibly
> hard. We had this vision that we could be a big company, but there was
> no obvious way to get there. The solution only presented itself when
> a friend pointed out to me that my business did not have to be big.
> Maybe it would be one day, but why don't you try and start small.

It was 2009, and the idea of selling online and connecting with
customers through platforms like Twitter was just starting to
emerge. The DTC revolution had begun, and Jane saw her chance
to be part of it.

Using their last bit of grant and investment money, Jane and her
team turned their testing lab into the most basic manufacturing plant,
got some help to design a website and came up with a brand name –
Sugru derives from 'súgradh', the Irish word for play. For the website,
they produced a product explainer video of Jane telling her story, and
made 1000 packs.

> When we launched, the only things we really had was a website and a
> video on the front page saying we have invented this new material, and
> we believe in fixing, making and modifying things. It was essentially if
> you believe in that, give it a go, and we would love to see what you do.
> It was a very open-ended piece of communication in that we weren't
> trying to convince people. It was more like we think this is useful and
> exciting. We wanted our customers to tell us what they could do with
> it, and that really kind of appealed to a more imaginative set of internet
> users who wanted to get their hands on the stuff and were happy to give
> us feedback.

Those initial 1000 packs sold out in six hours and were enough to
generate all kinds of excitement.

> We initially thought that the product would be used as we had around
> the house. We never anticipated how useful it would be to fix gadgets.

We were getting loads of pictures of people fixing broken bits of plastic, including on expensive things like laptop chargers, printers and kitchen appliances.

A better invention than the iPad and community-led marketing

The next part of their launch strategy was sending samples to bloggers and journalists for them to review. While most of them didn't bother, the ones who did gave them rave reviews, including a 10 out of 10 from a very influential journalist from *The Daily Telegraph*. The positive PR did not stop there; Sugru was featured in *Wired* magazine and was number 22 in *Time* magazine's 50 most useful inventions in 2010. High praise, considering the iPad was number 34 on the list.

PR was good, but the best marketing was being generated organically from the community of hackers and fixers using the product. Not only were Sugru's customers telling their friends about it, but they were also inspiring others by sharing how they were finding all sorts of new uses for the product. It was from this community that the product became famous for many weird and wonderful applications. Examples of fixing laptop cables, shoes, bathroom sinks and dishwasher racks were outdone by more inspired uses, including wheelchair enhancements, braille microwave buttons and even a one-legged chicken with a Sugru prosthetic limb. The marketing challenge had become how to balance using these more interesting and engaging examples with being most helpful by highlighting more obvious and regular applications. The answer was generally to let the community do the job for them. Jane explained:

> When we started, we had a hacker's mindset, 'hack things better' was our original slogan. It was a bit subversive, and we set out to attract people of a certain mindset. We genuinely wanted to learn from them, and that was very motivating for people. They really liked the idea of helping us.

Over time this community culture became embedded in all aspects of the brand's marketing. Even today, new ways of using the product are posted continuously onto community boards such as Pinterest as well as being shared via the Sugru website.

When retailers come knocking

The business that started small was becoming bigger. The question was, how big could they go? Having established a following in the hacker community, Sugru was now in that enviable position of having the retailers starting to knock on the door asking to stock their product. First up was Amazon. It's not always an easy choice to list on Amazon. There are fees, set-up admin and ongoing marketing costs to contend with. In addition, you may be cannibalizing your own more valuable DTC sales. But for Jane, it was necessary. 'Consumer preference, free shipping and sense of security that things will actually arrive meant that we should definitely do it. We put quite a lot of effort into it, but the volumes are so significant it's worth the work.' At the time of writing, Amazon remains one of Sugru's biggest sales channels, especially in the United States.

Then came bricks and mortar retail. One of the first and most interested parties, who wanted to stock, was the UK's largest home improvements retailer, B&Q. How could Jane and her team refuse their offer to put them on shelf? A listing with them was the chance to reach so many more people and get them to join their community of hackers and fixers. Sugru launched into 300 B&Q stores, and the team was able to tell the world they were more than just a DTC company.

The problem with retail

At this point, the Sugru story becomes less of a fairy tale and more of a grind. DTC is brilliant for connecting directly with the audience who understand and want your product. The beauty of the internet is so long as you put effort into your website, have good SEO and maybe run some targeted search ads (PPC), the dynamic is such that if you have a specialized offer, your customers will often find you rather than you trying to find them. However, offline things are very different. While the internet is infinite, shelf space is finite, which makes on-shelf real estate expensive.

The economics of a finite amount of shelf space is why there are often listing or slotting fees for new products. For new brands and products, the second challenge you face is changing the shopping habits of people in store, the majority of whom are never likely to have heard of you. Therefore being in retail means that as well as paying any fees you have to significantly ramp up your marketing efforts and change how you communicate and educate potential new customers. Gaining new customers is essential as you need to generate sales to justify your place in-store. The slotting fees buy you time, but listing your products needs to be profitable for the stores. Even in the biggest superstores, there are thousands of other products vying for your little bit of shelf space. Getting a listing is hard work, even if you are lucky enough to get a retail buyer asking for your products. Even trickier is maintaining a listing, especially when you are first to market with a new product and an unknown brand.

Sugru quickly found out they had to significantly increase their internal resources, including more specialist retail sales and marketing people. They also needed to have a much bigger marketing budget. Achieving this meant more external investment, which they obtained through crowdfunding from their community and borrowing cash to fund their expansion.

Getting access to more money is a shrewd move if the increased revenue arrives. But you have to hit your targets. More money to fund growth means more pressure, and if the sales numbers do not progress as planned, there are consequences.

The business found that even with a huge community of customers and fans, simply not enough people in store were picking up the product. The internet allows niches to thrive. However, in retail, it is usually the more mainstream products that are the ones that drive the sales and therefore justify their place on the shelf. After years of effort and investment, the company concluded they were better suited to stick with DTC as their primary sales channel. Retail was not all bad for Sugru though – they still generate significant revenue (around 10 per cent of total sales) via Target in the United States and Robert Dyas in the UK. However, the majority of listings were too hard and too expensive to sustain. Mainstream retail was not quite ready for Sugru, and they were not ready for it.

The efforts put into the bricks and mortar retail channel were nearly the undoing of the whole business. Jane explained:

> We took some big investment decisions around the potential of retail that turned out not to pan out in the long run. This turned out to be really risky for a business of our size. We got into a very precarious position as we were dependent on a certain sales pipeline coming through within retail. When these listings come in, they are chunky, offering a big step up in growth. However, if they don't come in it's a risk.

The cost of overstretching

Pushing hard into retail meant the business became overstretched financially, and this came to a head when their bank reduced their debt funding facility. Suddenly, the company was not able to service its debts.

Fortunately, all was not lost. In 2018 the German adhesive company, Tesa, bought the company and have invited Jane and her team to continue growing the business. As part of Tesa, Sugru has retained its independence, with Jane remaining at the helm. This independence makes sense as it is a new product for the Tesa family and has a different customer base. For these reasons, they have left Jane and her crew to carry on building the Sugru business with the focus on DTC channels.

The sale to Tesa has allowed Sugru to continue to provide their useful space-age rubber for the community of hackers, fixers and makers. However, the stretch into retail and subsequent financial strain also came at a cost to that precious group. When the company crowdfunded, many of their biggest fans and customers took the opportunity to invest in the business that made the products they loved. Investing in new businesses is always risky; however, crowd-funding also promotes more emotionally driven investments. The issue was that when the sale to Tesa happened, those crowdfund investors ended up making significantly less money from the exit than they had invested into the business.

Jane explained what happened:

> Joining forces with Tesa was positive for the business; however, it was a very big disappointment to me that our community who got behind us in the crowdfunding ended up having a negative experience. We felt it because these were some of our biggest fans, and maybe we could not fully explain what happened as well as we wanted.

Wisdom and the future

While Jane was unsurprisingly disappointed at how the retail experiment did not work out, she remains as enthusiastic as ever about the brand, product and their future. Sugru's new owners have also invested in launching a new and improved Sugru formula, as well as supporting their growth into other countries with a French and German language version of their DTC website. Today the repair movement is starting to gather pace with more and more people buying less and prolonging the life of the things they have. This repair and reuse mindset is at the heart of Sugru's DNA. While not everyone will be a fixer, Sugru remains a cheap and easy way to build confidence and get into the repair and modify mindset.

LESSONS FROM SUGRU

1 Take time to develop your product and get the help you need to get it right. Jane spent over six years refining her product until it was ready for launch. She demonstrated the need to be patient to get a product into the market that could do what she has designed it to do.

2 The starting small mindset allowed the team to get the company off the ground. When they realized licensing was not an option, turning their development lab into a little manufacturing plant, and designing a website and video was all they needed for a DTC launch. They knew they could be big, but there was nothing wrong with starting small.

3 Initially, they did not tell their customers how they should use the product. Instead, they told them it was exciting and asked their customers to tell them how they used it. This open-ended communication ended up as the best form of marketing. It was their customers that came up with the best and most memorable applications and then shared them with the rest of the community.

4 Sending products to prominent bloggers and journalists resulted in some stellar PR. While most samples and feedback requests were ignored, the recipients that liked it generated the press they needed to spread the word.

5 Going into retail requires a different set of skills and resources than DTC. Sugru took a big gamble on making retail work. When it did not work out as well as they had hoped, it put them in a precarious position. All new channels carry different amounts of risk and reward. They need to be correctly understood. Otherwise, you may find yourself unwittingly betting the farm.

6 Crowdfunding is a brilliant way to allow your biggest fans to invest in the business. However, if the business fails to make a return on that investment, those fans can become upset and frustrated with the company. Communication is critical; however, as Jane explained, not everything can be disclosed when a business is sold. Remember when your community invests in you, if you don't make good on that investment, you may hurt the ones who love you the most.

07

Using DTC toilet paper to build toilets and ensure access to sanitation for every person on the planet by 2050

Who Gives A Crap

Today you can buy just about anything at the click of a button. You can also usually sign up for a subscription service and never have to worry about running out again. The success of razor blade companies Dollar Shave Club, Harry's and Cornerstone provided the blueprint for a DTC subscription business. Find an essential everyday item, offer better quality, price and service, create an emotional connection through your brand and take away the stress and hassle of ordering again and again. In addition to razor blades, just about everything can be now bought via a DTC subscription. Household essentials like dishwasher tablets, flowers, toilet cleaners, socks, cosmetics, kids' puzzles, cheese, beer, wine, tea towels, bagels and even bacon are now available for slick and reliable home delivery.

It is easy to forget, the ease of finding subscription services for household products is still a relatively new experience. When Who Gives A Crap first launched in 2012, a DTC toilet roll business was a novel idea. Today, they compete with hundreds of other brands, including Reel, Biffy, Peach, Naked Sprout and services offered by traditional multinationals like Procter & Gamble and Kimberly-Clark. What is still unique about Who Gives A Crap is their business model and is the reason, amongst all this competition, they remain the main online destination for DTC toilet rolls.

A mission-led organization

Who Gives A Crap were founded in 2012 by Melburnian Simon Griffiths and his friends Danny Alexander and Jehan Ratnatunga. They were never a business launched to exploit the DTC trend. DTC happened by accident. The mission from their inception has been to give everyone in the world access to clean water and sanitation. They achieve this by donating 50 per cent of their profits to charitable partners. As of 2021, they have made more than A$20 million (Australian dollars) in profits, equating to over A$10 million in donations to partner projects mainly across Africa, India and East Asia. It's an inspiring and unusual business, as I found out when I met with co-founder and CEO Simon Griffiths to learn his story.

When I met with Simon in December 2019, little did we know how the world was about to change. Simon was sitting in his house in Melbourne, Australia, and at the time, it felt a little bit unusual to chat to him for a couple of hours over a Zoom call. Since then, a lot has changed, especially for Who Gives A Crap, one of the most worthy winners of the pandemic-induced switch to online purchases in 2020 and 2021.

Matching passion with productivity and impact

Like many of the other founders in the book, Simon's entrepreneurial leanings were evident as he grew up on Australia's west coast. He was generating cash by mowing lawns, lemonade stands and the like. Then, like many young Australians in their teens, he travelled to London. It was here at the age of 17 that he set up his first real business. When he discovered he had less than £100 left to his name, rather than heading back home, he taught himself how to build websites and started his own web development business. After a couple of successful years, this first business came to an end with the dot.com crash. So in 2001 he headed back to Australia to get a degree like the rest of his peers. He enrolled on an Electrical Engineering and Economics degree from the University of Melbourne. After that, things got a bit more conventional for a few years. Simon explained his situation:

> I pretty much felt like I had all of the entrepreneurial spirit drained
> out of me. At university, you get told you become an accountant or an
> investment banker or a management consultant. These are the jobs
> people kind of funnel you into, instead of saying, hey, maybe you'd be
> great at starting your own business. I felt like entrepreneurship and
> being a business person actually had a bit of a sort of negative spin to
> it, for whatever reason, back in the early 2000s. And so towards the end
> of my degree, with blinkers on, I got funnelled into some of these jobs.

Simon first became a disillusioned electrical engineer and then a disinterested investment banker and just about stopped himself becoming some sort of unfulfilled management consultant. Luckily he had worked out the problem.

> I realized if I haven't really enjoyed these other two jobs, which are
> similar to management consulting, then why would that be the right
> sort of career for me to go down? I realized the problem is that I'm
> not really passionate about the outcome of what I'm working on. And
> as a result, I can't get motivated or excited about what I'm doing,
> and therefore I'm only giving it sort of 60 or 70 per cent of everything
> that is possible. I reflected on that and said if I'm going to feel like I'm
> giving something my all, I need to find something where I really care
> about the outcome. And so I took a bit of a backflip and went to work
> in the non-profit sector.

The limitations of traditional not-for-profit models

Simon went to work for an education-based project in Africa but became frustrated when he realized that no matter how hard he worked, he could only ever help a small segment of the millions of people who needed assistance. His entrepreneurial instincts told him there must be a better way to help those in need. He came back to Australia and founded Shebeen, a not-for-profit bar that specializes in beers, wines and spirits from the developing world. The idea was that the business would send its proceeds back to those countries where the drinks came from for development projects. This foundational experience of setting up a charitable enterprise was an important stepping stone for Who Gives A Crap, and critically it informed how it should be structured.

> I realized that the Shebeen business model itself would always, again, be limited in its scale. Because it's a bricks and mortar business it is inherently difficult to scale. Even if we could run 10, 15 or 20 locations, we'd still never be able to generate the donations that would be necessary to solve some of the problems that we were looking at. So I started to consider what other products could we work with that someone can buy regardless of where they are. Unlike the bar, they don't need to live in the neighbourhood to come and experience the products. Also, the products should be relevant regardless of what their interests are. For example, they don't need to be someone that enjoys alcohol for this to make sense for them.

An epiphany 10 years in the making

It was contemplating this problem in the bathroom, staring at a roll of toilet paper, that inspiration hit. Simon realized the answer was selling toilet paper to build toilets. Simon explained that moment of inspiration:

> It was a moment that was 10 years in the making. I had been on a creative journey to discover the things that I really loved and was passionate about. I also understood that if I wasn't working on things that I truly believed in, I couldn't be efficient with my time and wouldn't achieve everything that I could. The journey to get to that point took

10 years, but then the final idea was the epiphany of walking into the bathroom, seeing some toilet paper and being like, holy shit, this is a great idea.

As well as his passion for making a difference, Simon was also acutely aware of the size of the problem. He discovered that 60 per cent of the global population took their access to proper sanitation for granted, leaving the other 40 per cent to suffer. While things were slowly improving, at the current rate of change, it would take at least until 2085 for everyone to have access to a toilet.

> It seemed mind-boggling. Crazy that for the most basic of human needs, we could not provide that at a pace that seemed anywhere near reasonable. And so there was just this opportunity to work with products that we all know and need and use the proceeds to help people in need. It would provide the perfect link of brand, products and cause coming together to create something that would help to motivate customers in a way that no one has ever done before.

Finding a way not to have to rely on exclusively philanthropic donations

The next problem to solve was one Simon had encountered at Shebeen. When raising money for the bar as it was not for profit, investors could only ever receive a social return. There would be no equity, no dividend payment and no exits. Simon discovered that it was hard to find that particular type of person who was willing to invest in the business, knowing they would never get their money back.

> Running a non-profit bar made me realize the limitations of the 100 per cent profit donation model. So we decided to switch it up to a 50 per cent profit donation model. We thought that structure would make a much more sustainable business. And as a result, we believe we could be more than twice as big this way, and therefore, we could have more impact by just donating half of our profits instead of 100 per cent of them. And then the other part of it was we wanted to show the business existed

because of a social problem. And if that problem wasn't there, then we wouldn't be selling toilet paper. We felt like 50 per cent was a big enough number to tell that side of the story, but also allows the benefit of being able to build the business in a more sustainable, scalable manner.

Crowdfunding the idea and going viral

Even with a structure for investors to get involved, not many wanted to take the risk. It was a new venture with a new way of doing business. So to get going, they relied on a small grant, which they spent on getting to the United States to set up a product crowdfunding campaign to see what people really thought of the idea. In July 2012, the company launched an IndieGoGo campaign titled 'Who Gives A Crap – toilet paper that builds toilets'. Inspired by the Dollar Shave Club 'Our Blades Are F***ing Great' video launched a few months before, they wanted to come up with a campaign that could go viral. Eventually, they settled on the idea of live streaming Simon sitting on the toilet until they had reached their $50,000 target. The money was to pay for their first batch of toilet rolls. Their pledges would receive not only toilet rolls but, depending on how much they paid, would also receive live shout outs, stickers, badges, t-shirts and even their name printed on the first edition packs.

The campaign was so original that it achieved its goal of going viral. That Simon was sitting on a toilet to raise money for more toilets was picked up by news outlets worldwide. Interview requests and social media coverage meant that Simon was required to stick to his task until finally, after 50 hours, the funding target was met. Apart from some damage to Simon's legs – he now advises anyone not to sit on a toilet for 50 hours – the campaign was a success. In addition to now having the money to make some products, the campaign also showed them there was a big demand for their idea and that it had global appeal.

The initial idea was for the primary market to be the United States; however, during the IndieGoGo campaign, the majority of the interest had come from Australia. So rather than going first for the US market, after they had fulfilled their initial campaign commitments, they decided to initially focus exclusively on Australia. They would eventually re-establish operations in the United States in 2017, also launching in the UK the same year.

Choosing DTC instead of dealing with supermarkets

In the beginning, the business was not considering online as their primary sales channel.

> At this point in time, we thought that the distribution channel would be supermarkets, as 99.9 per cent of Australia's toilet paper was sold in supermarkets. We thought that online would give us some small sales but would never be a core channel. At this point, no one had ever sold toilet paper online before. It was when we sold out, of what we thought would be three months of stock, in just five days that we started to take online more seriously.

At this time, Simon also found out that retailers worked at a different pace to what can be achieved digitally and that they were also less receptive to innovation.

> We thought supermarkets would be key, but after 18 months of conversations about a trial across 18 stores, the buyer stopped returning our calls. We then found out they had become the seafood buyer. They eventually introduced us to the new buyer, and we had to start again. Then one of the first things the buyer told us was they were reducing the number of brands in store, which made it much less likely we would get a listing. We thought you know what, our business had been growing in the background without a retail listing, and we did not want to enter into a margin war to win market share. So we put conversations with retailers on hold and decided to focus all our efforts on a direct to consumer business.

Keeping costs low with organic marketing

With the focus on DTC and generating a maximum amount of profit every year, the business has always been determined that it would be the product and the mission that would do most of the marketing for them. Customer acquisition had to be low cost. To achieve this, in addition to linking the product to the mission, it also looks very different from most toilet paper you would find in the supermarket. The rolls are made from either bamboo or recycled paper. Both are more environmentally friendly than mass-market alternatives. Rather than coming in plastic bags, the rolls are wrapped in paper, and it is through this wrap, the brand has fun with colours, personalization and themes. Limited editions have included where's the loo (think Where's Wally), a play edition and special Christmas paper wrapped rolls. Their customers were encouraged to give these prewrapped gifts to their friends as a Christmas present. A thoughtful, different gift and another way to spread the word about the business and its mission.

Simon describes their light-hearted marketing strategy as 'hopefully something that makes our customers have a giggle and then want to tell someone else the facts that they've learnt [about the mission]. Our number one marketing channel is organic.'

They also have tools to work out the correct quantity and frequency for your household to set up a subscription. However, if you are the sort of person who likes to buy at the last moment, they also include a few bright red 'emergency rolls' at the bottom of each box to indicate things are about to become problematic and a new order is due.

While the products look great and have sustainability credentials, the best form of marketing still relates to the connection to the company purpose: to provide everyone in the world access to a toilet by 2050. 'You need to be really authentic and have a truthful brand story. With this, you can put the brand in front of everything you do.' The combination of well made, good looking, sustainable products, which contribute to a bigger mission, has helped the word spread, and the company has grown exponentially. They have added more products to the range, including kitchen roll, tissues and cleaning cloths. They have also extended their distribution beyond Australia, the United States and the UK and added warehouses into Canada and the Netherlands (to serve the rest of Europe).

Growing 40× in a single day

From 2013 to 2019 the company has doubled in size each year. That was until 2020. Demand began to skyrocket in the spring of that year as COVID-19 pre-lockdown panic buying set in. At the start of March 2020, with the public fearing supply chain shortages and the inability to get their groceries, toilet rolls were piled into shopping carts resulting in empty supermarket shelves. The surge happened very quickly. Customers who had not considered buying online before started to sign up, and within 24 hours, sales had doubled. The day after that, there was a five-fold increase, and by day four, the panic resulted in sales nearly 40 times higher than what had been a typical day's sales just a month before.

Of course, nobody had anticipated this increase in demand. As their stock ran low, the company had to stop new customers signing up as they tried to ensure they had enough paper to serve their existing customers. The panic-buying phenomenon was not localized to one area or country, and they stocked out in every region (Australia, the UK and the United States). Simon began hiring new people to deal with the increased interest. They now had half a million people on their waiting list, and they were also working around the clock as they tried to rebuild their stocks. While it was a difficult time, it also proved to be the perfect moment to make more sales and help new customers understand what the business was about and sign them up (as soon as stock allowed).

Record donations but still not enough

While the pandemic has been challenging, some good has come out of it. In particular, the increased demand for Who Gives A Crap products has enabled them to donate more to their causes than ever before. In 2013 the annual charitable donation was A$2500. In 2017, the amount had risen to A$746k. The increased sales in 2020 allowed them to double the total of all of their previous donations combined, allowing them to send a whopping A$5.85 million to their charitable partners. Things calmed down a bit in 2021; however, with the help of new customers and increased awareness, they could still donate A$2.5 million, meaning in eight years, total donations were over A$10 million.

As we have seen in some of the other businesses in this book, high growth often means deferred profits. I asked Simon how he managed this, especially as they relied on annual profits for the donations. He told me, 'Early on, one of our advisors lent us $50,000 to pay off our production costs. When we paid this back in just five months, he said if we ever wanted more money, he would be happy to help.' So the business got into a regular cycle of taking on debt to make the stock and then paying the debt back, in full, and making a donation by the end of the tax year. This model had seen them through their first eight years. By following a very disciplined approach of managing cash flow and keeping costs low, they have impressively managed to be both high growth and high profit.

The problem is that while they can continue this way, the business needs to accelerate to achieve its goals. Simon explained:

> So we're now in a position where we could continue growing without changing the business and strategy. But we also want to make sure that everyone in the world has access to a toilet. And there are 2 billion people that don't have access to a toilet. So we recognize that if we're going to hit our target, we need to think about how we grow the business with new sales channels, new geography, new products, and that all requires potentially rethinking what our capital strategy looks like. And because we've got the 50 per cent model, we can turn to equity.

Using their equity to accelerate growth

In September 2021, the business announced they had used some of the 50 per cent equity available for a Series A investment round. Like most things with Who Gives A Crap, the funding round was different from a typical Series A. The business had some very stringent criteria for any potential investors. (1) Any investor has to be aligned with the mission, (2) they must have expertise in developing consumer brands and (3) critically must be what Simon calls 'patient capital'. Patient capital means their investors had to align themselves with the company's 30-year mission to provide toilets and sanitation for everyone in the world. The longer-term approach quickly removed many traditional institutions as they tend to look for a return in a five- to seven-year horizon. The 'patient capital' releases any pressure to produce a quick return on investment. Instead, their partners need to be in it for the long term and allow Simon and his co-founders to use the capital to grow the business in the way they think is best.

After eight and a half years of being in the unusual position of being high growth and self-funded, Who Gives A Crap have successfully found a group of investors to match their funding criteria and raised a total of A\$40 million. The company will use this money to extend into new countries, introduce new products and grow the business. It also releases them from their debt cycle obligations reducing risk and lowering cost. With money in the bank, to grow and be more efficient, expect bigger and bigger annual donations as Who Gives A Crap works to complete its sanitation mission by 2050.

LESSONS FROM WHO GIVES A CRAP

1 Simon spent 10 years finding a way to create a business where he could use his skills to work on something he truly believed in. Finding something that was genuinely motivating meant that he could work to his maximum output.

2 By working in the not-for-profit sector, Simon identified what he needed to fix with the Who Gives A Crap business model. He first realized he needed a product and business he could sufficiently scale. He also worked out that to give themselves the best chance of success and hence have the most significant impact, they should not have to rely on philanthropic donations. The answer was a business with 50 per cent of the profits retained and 50 per cent donated to their mission.

3   Because the business needed to generate annual profits, they used their cash restraints to an advantage. They knew they would have to keep costs low, so they used the product as the primary marketing source. A great example of this is the Christmas wrapped roll for holiday gifts. Being disciplined and keeping costs low while they grew the business resulted in both growth and profits.

4   That they had been able to use rapidly repaid loans to self-fund the company for the first eight years meant that when they raised Series A, they knew exactly what they were looking for from investors. Waiting also meant they had more time to develop the business and brand, increasing its valuation.

5   A strict framework for investors ensures they have teamed up with the right ones to help and support their mission with no conflict of interest or pressure for quick returns.

08

Building a community
for a higher purpose

TRIBE

The challenges launching a brand

When we started Peppersmith, we were still using the traditional model for introducing retail products. The way to take a new product to market had a standard formula. If you were a large company, you would spend years identifying a niche and formulating a product to fulfil that unmet need. Once you had done that, you would agree to some listings with the retailers, generally with the promise of some intensive marketing, most often in the form of television advertising. If you were a small company, like us, this was not an option. Instead, you would seed the product into smaller independent stores and begin to build awareness on the shelf and slowly but surely, as more people were buying the product, you could get it onto more shelves until, eventually, you could agree a listing with the bigger retailers. Whatever the size of your company, both these routes were full of uncertainty and risk. If you were a big brand, you would spend years in development, spend a fortune on advertising more often than not to discover consumers did not like your innovation, and the product would be pulled from the shelves. In the second scenario, while you are not investing the equivalent amounts of cash, you invest heavily in time. It can take years to build distribution in smaller stores, and even if you can prove your worth to get listed in a major retailer, you may find yourself competing with products backed by those brands with millions available to promote their wares. The choice of having to spend vast amounts of time and money for uncertain returns was becoming a significant barrier. Launching products had became the domain of the very rich, brave or naive.

Thankfully, just when you may have felt that launching products has become too hard and too risky, DTC has radically lowered these barriers of entry. Anyone with an idea for a product can start on DTC, where you can test product appeal quickly, and you can also make sure it gets in front of the people most likely to buy it. This targeting is done either by social media targeting or SEO-optimized websites. This is a big step forward and something I wished we had considered when we started Peppersmith, but even then, we were still in the world of internet v 1.0. The Web 2.0, which began around 2007, is all about social connections. Social media and social media advertising is part of this, but for brands, there is something even better than merely connecting, which is community building. If you can build a community before you launch, you will have a much better chance of success. A community is important because you will know the members well and critically know what they want. Furthermore, this community will be made up of your biggest fans. They will be hungry for your new products and will also be there to support you as you grow.

In my conversations with the best DTC brands around, the importance of building a community has already been mentioned. One of the best examples of the benefits of community building is TRIBE, a UK-based sports and nutrition business. The TRIBE community supports the brand, and in return, TRIBE provides that community with products they need.

A tribe of runners

I caught up with Tom Stancliffe (a third of the TRIBE founding team) to find out how this works. When I spoke to Tom, I was in my regular seat, at home, on yet another pandemic-forced video call. Tom, on the other hand, wasn't at a computer screen at all – he was taking my call from London's Victoria Park, where he'd ventured out for his daily head-clearing walk. As a result, our conversation was accompanied by chirping birds rather than the now all too familiar pings and bings from our computers and phones. Hearing the tranquillity made me think, I want a piece of that action, which is just the point. Tom and his team have built a community by getting people active and outdoors, and in turn, they've also built a business out of selling products to that community. One action mutually reinforcing the other.

That joy of getting outdoors and a shared love of ultra running first brought the TRIBE team together. Consisting of co-founders Tom, Guy Hacking and Rob Martineau, the group of two ex-lawyers and a banker have escaped the city to follow their passion. TRIBE started out wanting to be the 'graze for runners', but their success has been less about identifying a niche and far more about connecting people, giving back and enjoying what they do.

The business was built on a love of running but also driven on by a more noble cause. It all started back in 2012. The team wanted to test their running abilities by entering the legendary Marathon des Sables, a six-day, 156-mile race across the Sahara desert in North Africa. The MDS, as it is known among the adventure race community, is not just about enduring the heat and covering the distance. You are also required to carry everything you need to survive on your back. It is not for the faint of heart or weary of legs. Tom, Guy and Rob are made of strong stuff.

After all three had successfully completed the gruelling race, they found out that they had what it took to tough it out in the most extreme conditions. More importantly, they also discovered that events like the MDS were a fantastic way to raise money for charity.

In his role as a lawyer, Tom had been working with an organization called The Centre of Social Justice, which was giving legal support to the victims of child trafficking and modern-day slavery. It was a cause the whole team had become passionate about. After getting significant charitable sponsorship, for this cause, for their efforts in the Marathon De Sables, they discovered they could use their love of ultra running as a way of driving awareness and raising money for a worthy cause. With this end in mind, they decided to create an event of their own.

In 2013 Tom, Guy and Rob set off from Odessa in Ukraine for a 1000-mile run across Eastern Europe to the Croatian city of Dubrovnik. They dubbed the event 'The Run for Love'. The race can be pinpointed as the real starting point of everything the business has achieved since. More than 250 runners joined them over the 30 days it took them to finish the race. They ended up raising a total of £250,000 to help pay for a safe house for the victims of child trafficking.

The problem with Mars bars

During this race, they discovered a problem with how they fuelled themselves over those long 1000 miles. Tom explained:

> At the end of that amazing experience, we had learnt a lot about ourselves. We also learned a lot about the nutrition you needed to train and compete in these ultra-long activities. We thought it would be amazing to take the learnings around our community of athletes, adventurers and anyone who enjoyed being active.

So it was the three friends decided they would set up a nutrition-focused business and crucially use it as a platform to help further the cause of fighting modern-day slavery. With this goal in mind, they quit their well-paid city jobs to create TRIBE. It was a brave leap, but by this stage, the team were used to out-sized challenges.

TRIBE was a company that set out to sell more healthy, plant-based sports nutrition products to athletes like themselves. Tom described the problem with sports nutrition:

> During our training and races, we found that when it came to sports supplements and performance fuel, we had to rely on highly synthetic, badly branded products. Even though this was when the vegan movement was becoming embraced by the running community, we often found ourselves standing at the side of the road, having to eat a Mars bar or some horrible sports gel. We wanted to have something more natural, tasty and nutritious to give us our energy.

All this happened in an era when modern sports science and books, including *New York Times* bestseller, *Born to Run*, began championing the benefits of simple diets, including lots of nuts and seeds. The science was being backed up when many athletes, like the legendary Scott Jurek, started winning ultra races fuelled by a 100 per cent vegan diet. Despite this, the TRIBE team had discovered first hand that for most amateur and recreational runners, sugar, fat and dairy were often the only things readily available to power up your weary limbs. Thus TRIBE designed their products to be a more natural, plant-based tastier alternative to traditional sports supplements and on-the-go snacks.

As well as selling products, Tom and the team were also focused on building a community of recreational, amateur and professional athletes. They did this by creating events that could also be the basis for their charitable contributions. These events were anything from a 30-minute lunchtime training run for fewer than 10 people, to bigger 5 km and 10 km events, adventure races, all the way up to major multistage multiday races. Tom went on to explain:

> We would never have considered the product without the community and vice versa. We saw it as a holistic offering – with the product fulfilling a need, giving us the platform to create events and build the community, and using the community and events to raise money for the charity.

The TRIBE flywheel

The more products they sold, the more events they could hold, and more events meant more money raised for charity and more publicity to help grow the business. If the company grew, they could continue to do it again, but bigger and better each time. This type of virtuous cycle is an excellent example of the flywheel model first explained by author Jim Collins in his book *Good to Great* and championed by Jeff Bezos at Amazon. At Amazon, the flywheel works where a great customer experience drives traffic, the traffic then attracts brands who want to sell on the platform, which builds a better selection, which then brings in even more customers. As the company grows, it can also improve its systems and further lower costs, making the flywheel spin even faster. Similarly, at TRIBE, their products, events, community and charity reinforce and propel each other, allowing each touchpoint to help fuel the whole business and move it forward.

Like many DTC brands, the initial products were of humble origins. Tom revealed that the first products had been conceived in Rob's mum's kitchen. Once they had the initial concepts, they then worked with professional product developers and nutritionists to get them up to scratch and ready for launch. The first products to be introduced were energy bars and trail mixes. Once the products were ready, they needed a platform to start selling. Running events seemed an excellent place to start, but they soon discovered they couldn't be at every event. They also realized that even if they could be at all the events, runners also needed the products throughout their training and not just on race day. They needed another way. DTC was the obvious answer because it made products accessible to consumers wherever they were. It also allowed personalization to tailor their mix of products depending on their sport, taste preferences and training regimes. You could buy products for fuel, protein or recovery, and, importantly, you had the ability to mix them depending on your athletic needs and taste preferences. Lastly, DTC meant it was also easy to offer a subscription service, which meant TRIBE customers could effortlessly receive a regular supply to fuel them before, during and after their activities.

With products developed, the brand designed and a DTC platform set up, TRIBE officially launched in 2015. Initially, the brand did their marketing through events that they either set up or via other people's races and sponsored events. Cleverly, the sponsorship was usually paid for by selling products to these events at a discounted price. Selling their products in this way allowed the brand to drive awareness and sample products with minimal overheads. The team also used their running credentials and growing community to partner with some real fitness heavyweights, like Nike and Lululemon, and they did this from a very early stage. These affiliate partnerships gave the brand a real boost. Not only did they allow them access to a broader audience, they also were able to associate their brand and what they stood for with these much better known and loved companies. This association gave TRIBE increased credibility and awareness.

It was about six months after the business launched, in January 2016, when things really started taking off. TRIBE had done an excellent job of creating brand credibility and awareness through its events and partnerships. All this meant that when they turned on targeted social media advertising that first January, they were top of mind for the many people who had made a New Year's resolution to improve their health and fitness. Even though they were a small DTC company, their affiliation with the Nike and Lululemons of the world made them seem much more established than they were.

Sales grew quickly throughout 2016 as they attracted more customers to what they could offer. To support this growth, they added more products while the team refined their marketing messages and improved the ordering experience. With the foundations laid, they were ready to ramp things up further.

It was time for another epic event, the Run for Love II, another multistage ultra-adventure race. The ambition was for it to be even longer, have more participants and raise even more money for the anti-slavery cause than the original Run for Love. Run for Love II was a duathlon (running and cycling). The cycling part was intentional as the products had now also been adopted by cyclists seeking the same benefits as the running community. This time, the race covered exactly 2000 km (1250 miles) across eight countries from Sarajevo, in Bosnia Herzegovina, to London. Again, like the original Run for Love, the TRIBE community joined in, either running the whole thing or joining for particular sections of the race. The event culminated in hundreds of TRIBE runners completing the last 20-mile stretch along the North Downs, just south of London. The event successfully introduced even more people to the products, the brand and the community. It also raised another £250,000 for their charity.

A tribe of investors

Having a pre-built community has clear benefits for brand loyalty, brand awareness and product development. As we have already seen with Sugru and Cornerstone, the other benefit of a community is a small army of willing investors.

Before 2011, if a company wanted to raise cash, they would have to look for a hard-to-get business loan. Even if you successfully convinced a lender to give you money, those lenders would often place significant obligations on the founders to guarantee the loan repayment. If not a loan, your alternative was to look for venture capital. Or, if you were looking for more modest sums, you could find angel investors who had the money, expertise and appetite to seed an early-stage company. With the exception of being a close friend or family member of the founders, if you were a regular person (i.e. without a high net worth or access to the financial system), you would not traditionally get access to these sorts of investment opportunities. This restriction was removed in the early 2010s in the United States and Europe, where a new type of investment began to be allowed, equity crowdfunding. Equity crowdfunding is not to be confused with product crowdfunding platforms like Kickstarter, where the investment is primarily in return for a new product to be made. Equity crowdfunding means anybody could register with an approved platform to invest directly into companies seeking investment. The introduction of crowdfunding was a game-changer for regular smaller scale investors who can now quickly and simply invest any amount into businesses that previously they would not have had access to. It was also great for companies to be able to pitch their businesses to a wider audience and not have to rely on convincing angels or VCs to write very large cheques. Marketing savvy companies can also use a crowd fundraising round as a PR exercise to raise their profile and make these new investors cheerleaders for the business and brand.

The perfect combination is when consumers and fans of the business who have already invested emotionally into the brand can also put in their cash. As well as supporting the brand, investors could also be rewarded with a future financial gain.

'Even though we had lots of private investment offers, crowdfunding was a no-brainer for us,' recalled Tom.

> Consumer brand businesses tend to do well on crowdfunding as the products resonate with a wider audience, and then doubly so as we were such a community-led business. We thought it made sense and would be amazing that our community would also be able to own some of the business.

His instincts proved correct. The TRIBE community were indeed eager to invest. The initial crowdfund target of £1 million was smashed within days of the campaign launch. With their target reached, and though they did not necessarily need more money, they extended the round to ensure that as many of their community as possible had the opportunity to buy a stake. Eventually, they closed the round at nearly £1.8 million of investment from 1740 individual investors.

The money raised went towards building the team, developing the product range, investing in the website and brand building. However, they also had another critical goal to achieve – they needed to move away from being a subscription-only DTC business quickly and create an omnichannel offering.

Going beyond their niche

A DTC route was perfect in that it would allow TRIBE to easily connect with and cater for endurance runners and cyclists who needed a personalized nutrition plan. The problem was that there was a finite number of people who matched that criteria. Furthermore, training and races are followed by a recovery period where subscriptions would be paused or cancelled. There were lots of people who were using the products, the problem was they were not using them all the time. TRIBE catered brilliantly for a specific niche, but that niche was not big enough to sustain the business.

They needed scale. To do this, Tom and the team began to work on establishing TRIBE in retail stores as an on-the-go snack option.

In addition to their subscription service, they started allowing one-off purchases on both the website and on their store page on Amazon. Once the retail-ready products had been developed and the packaging updated, the team started to pitch to the retailers. Energy bars and sports nutrition are among the most crowded and competitive categories in food and drink. Despite this, their story, their active community and their focus on making the best possible products convinced the retail buyers to give TRIBE a chance. They gained listings first in UK health and wholefood chains, including Whole Foods Market, Planet Organic and Holland & Barrett. They then launched into the more mainstream retailers, including online supermarket Ocado, WHSmith Travel stores and, crucially, the grocery chain Sainsbury's.

According to Tom, this was a shrewd move. 'Going omnichannel has been a great decision, it's made the business stronger and more profitable. Ultimately the economics of running a subscription-only business was not going to work for us. It has been a brilliant thing to launch first into e-commerce and then retail.'

This scenario is a common dilemma for many DTC brands. DTC is fantastic at serving a particular niche. The problems arrive when that niche is too small to cover a business's operating costs or meet its organizational ambitions. For this reason, it is worth working out strategically whether your business will be pureplay DTC, omnichannel where DTC is just one revenue stream or if DTC is primarily used as a marketing tool. All these approaches are discussed in this book. You should also plan for what you might do if your initial assumptions are wrong, e.g. for when like TRIBE, you overestimated the market size of people who would benefit from a subscription box.

The increased revenue and profitability generated by the addition of retail channels gave the business the confidence to return to their community to raise more growth capital. In 2019 they raised a further £1.4 million via a new crowdfunding campaign from another 1165 investors. This time the money was to be used to continue to support their retail growth and expand into Europe via both the DTC model and local retailers.

Unsurprisingly, because of COVID-19 2020 didn't shape up as planned for TRIBE. Luckily, their e-commerce foundations and DTC expertise allowed them to weather the storm. In addition, to have been designed as a DTC business – meaning that they knew how to accommodate new customers who wanted to product to their door – the business also benefited from the broader changes to our lifestyles during this period. With everyone stuck at home, the lockdowns saw increased demand for health and fitness products, including TRIBE. The increased demand was serviced from their DTC channels and meant that the business continued to grow even with lower than planned retail sales.

Using their mission to motivate

Tom and the team have learnt a lot about building brands, developing products and running an omnichannel business. However, it is still the love of adventure and the determination to end modern-day slavery that spurs them on. From every TRIBE product sold, 1p is donated to the TRIBE Freedom Foundation. The Foundation is a stand-alone charity created to make it easier to raise funds and channel donations to support its mission to end modern-day slavery. The TRIBE events and races remain the core vehicle to drive donations to the Foundation and raise awareness of its purpose.

When talking about the Foundation, an animated Tom said, 'The charity is what gives us a purpose and reason for doing what we do. It also gives everyone involved a real sense of ownership and satisfaction as it [the Foundation] continues to grow and develop.'

As the best way to raise money and awareness for the Foundation is events, the team continue to focus on races and training events, both big and small. The third Run for Love took place in 2019 – this time a 253 km race across the volcanoes of the Azores, raising another £150k. The publicity generated around the event also helped with that year's crowdfunding.

The equity investments are helping grow the business and enable them to make better products to keep us healthy. They'll then use the brand to keep us fit by staging more training and race events, and they'll continue to use the events as a platform to raise money for their Foundation. To date, the team have raised over £1 million for the charity, and with more products and retailers on the horizon, TRIBE has built a robust business model that admirably serves a larger cause.

LESSONS FROM TRIBE

1 Create a community. The TRIBE community allows the business to understand its customers and what products they need. The community has helped build the brand and driven awareness and credibility. The company continues to create events for that community to attend and has also turned those community members into an army of cheerleading investors.

2 Tom, Guy and Rob focused on a problem they had and were passionate about (the lack of healthy and easily accessible training and recovery food and snacks for endurance athletes). They also harnessed a growing trend (plant-based fuel for athletes and exercise).

3 They used their mission of eradicating modern-day slavery as the ultimate motivation for the business. This aim incentivized the team way more than just building a business for a profit.

4 TRIBE have created a flywheel where each part of the business powers the next. Their products, events, community and charity support, reinforce and propel each other forward.

5 Changing course when they realized the niche they were serving was not big enough to sustain their business. For TRIBE this meant selling into retail stores and adopting an omnichannel model. The omnichannel approach also helped them when retail sales crashed during the 2020 pandemic. Having other channels (DTC and Amazon) to sell their product allowed them to grow even during this challenging time.

09

Launching a DTC brand in the 2020s. The new rules of the game

Lick | Clearing

Over the last few chapters, we have discussed the advantages of launching a product with a DTC strategy. First, there are fewer barriers of entry; for example, no retail buyer is deciding you are not the next big thing and denying you a place on the shelf. Second, DTC allows you to test, iterate and innovate more quickly and cheaply. Third, DTC allows you to build a direct relationship with your customers and find out what you need to do to serve them better, and by looking after their interests, you build trust and loyalty.

There is always a catch

If you think this sounds too good to be true, you are wise to be looking for the catch. We saw in the Cornerstone chapter that the landscape has changed considerably over the last decade. Competition is more abundant, the cost of acquiring customers has increased and consumer expectations are higher. The DTC brands that had come before and succeeded in changing consumers' buying habits and choices have set the bar high. Just turning up is no longer going to be a winning strategy.

If you don't (or can't) spend lots of cash to promote your new product, your best bet is to find a significant unmet need (e.g. Snag tights) or focus on a smaller niche, like Sugru. The challenge is that most brands are not trying to provide a completely revolutionary product or service (these are hard to find), but they are trying to invent a better mousetrap. Most successful companies are focused on finding a way to give customers a better deal and more value. This improved value could be via a better product (e.g. improved quality, more choice, personalization or enhanced sustainability credentials). It could mean quicker and more effective customer service or it could mean lower costs. The problem is that today improvement in a single dimension may not be enough to overcome the inertia caused by customers not wanting to take the risk of switching from their current solution. A combination of a better product, a better service and better value is needed to convince consumers that they should take the plunge, break their habits and try something new.

This chapter highlights not one but two newer DTC startups (one launched in 2020 and one in 2021). Both companies are not trying to innovate with revolutionary new products, for what they sell already exists. Instead, they are trying to radically change the rules in their prospective industries to give their customers a better experience and a better deal.

An excellent example of what it takes to launch a DTC brand in the 2020s is Lick, a UK home decor business established in 2020 by Lucas London and his co-founder, Sam Bradley. I met with Lucas a few months after the official launch of Lick. Other companies in this book are successful by innovating on data management, customer service, knowing your customer and using DTC to give you an advantage over the bricks and mortar brands. Where most differ from Lick is that they were all established five or more years ago. From Luke, I wanted to know the rules for launching a DTC brand now not then.

I learnt from Lucas that nowadays a brand needs to connect with its customers without solely relying on Facebook ads to find its audience. As Lucas told me, 'You have to get your brand, product and service spot on, and if you still have to rely on paid-for acquisition, you are going to run into problems.'

The rising costs of digital advertising

The problem with paid-for acquisition is that digital real estate has become expensive. What's more, even if you can afford to appear on someone's Facebook or Instagram feed, you must work hard to get them to look at your ad, and your ad needs to be exceptionally crafted and targeted to make someone act on what they have seen. This effort was not always the case. A few years ago, buying social ads, particularly on Facebook, was a very cost-effective way of attracting new customers. Social adverts were relatively novel so they would be less likely to be ignored, plus they were inexpensive. Nowadays, this is not the case; ads are everywhere, and they have become a costly way of showing off your wares. The price has increased due to the demand from brands big and small. For smaller brands, it is one of the only mediums with which they can afford to advertise. Furthermore, prominent brands have also entered the fray as they discover that the old ways of reaching customers (e.g. television ads) are no longer as effective.

What has happened with social ads in the 2010s is very similar to website banner advertising in the late 1990s. When banner ads were first introduced in the mid-1990s, they could get click-through rates of nearly 50 per cent. This did not last, and within a few years they lost their effectiveness, and their power has continued to diminish. According to a recent Think with Google study, the average click-through rate of display ads across all formats and placements is now 0.6 per cent.

When digital advertising gets more expensive, this increases customer acquisition costs (CAC). The ever-increasing pressure on CAC and the effectiveness of digital advertising have resulted in many DTC casualties. For example, if you checked your Facebook feed in 2015, you had an excellent chance of seeing an advert for the modern slipper brand Mahabis. Mahabis had award-winning products that looked and felt good. After launching in 2014, they quickly became very profitable by utilizing Facebook to attract new customers to buy their slippers. For the first few years, things were rosy. But as more and more brands were looking to move to digital ads, Facebook changed the pricing structure of their ad platform, and disaster struck for Mahabis. When Facebook changed their advertising structure, their CAC shot up, and profits became losses. The business could not adapt quickly enough and eventually went into administration and new ownership in 2018. Mahabis still exists as a DTC brand today, and if you are looking for some slippers, you should check them out. However, you will need to search a bit harder as you are significantly less likely to find them on your social feed.

What has changed is best illustrated in the DTC mattress market. First came Casper offering DTC convenience, modernity and value to a very old fashioned and unloved market. Unfortunately for Casper, when competitors started to enter the market, digital ad prices increased. The price increase was due to the bidding process structure operated by the platforms. Newer brands could and often did bid more to try and capture attention. Prices were further inflated as social media companies realized they could make even more money by charging more. The cost of advertising increased the costs of acquiring customers, making profits very hard to find for the mattress brands and many other DTC companies.

DTC brands now have to do things so much better than before. Therefore, to be successful, Lick needed to be more than a DTC paint business. If it launched five years ago, it might have been content with that. Not so today. Lucas told me:

> It was important to us that we don't just create a DTC paint brand. There are now a number of DTC paint brands out there across the US and Europe, and they have to raise lots of money to spend on Google Adwords and Facebook. They are playing the mattress game again. We plan to create barriers by having a large product range [beyond paint] and making something that has traditionally been frustrating, enjoyable. We want to support the decorator, inspire them and give confidence.

Removing the pain from decorating

For Lick, paint is only one part of the offer. Despite Lick being only a few months old, it already sells paint, wallpaper, a host of decorating accessories and has just launched a range of blinds. They also give advice, inspiration and online tools via their website. They do this by a combination of chat services, blog posts and a community of interior decorating fanatics guaranteed to inspire.

It may seem they have their work cut out with multiple products and services. However, Lucas was also keen to point out that they are also trying to simplify things.

> Currently, when it comes to paint, there is way too much choice. The traditional brands pride themselves on having all these different shades, but they are essentially asking you to choose a perfect blue from 50 slightly different blues. You wouldn't choose clothes like that. Our approach is to curate a small set of colour palettes which work for both the homeowner and for trade professionals.

As well as limiting colours, they have also removed all the different paint types by creating paint that can be used on multiple surfaces.

While they have a beautiful website full of pictures of idyllic-looking rooms, Lucas is determined that the brand should appeal to and be used by the mainstream consumer.

> There is a common misconception that you can now buy paint cheaply. The problem is that often it's poor quality, meaning you need twice as much. It also gets marked easily and does not carry the depth of colour. And if that's the case, you are getting poor value for money.

He continued, 'We have positioned ourselves for the mass market to make sure we are both affordable and good value.'

The affordability of the products is also critical for Lick's service to professional decorators and builders called Lick Pro. Lick Pro customers receive trade discounts (mainly due to the volume they buy), and shortly they will also be able to enjoy same-day delivery and order via an SMS service on their phone. If you have ever employed a decorator to paint a few walls, you will have likely experienced the frustration that some of the time paid for a skilled tradesperson is for them to go to the hardware store to buy the paint. Same-day home delivery removes that problem, which is more efficient for the decorator and saves money for the homeowner.

The importance of branding

Having a great looking brand might lead to the misconception of premium prices; however, their brand image has always been at the heart of everything they do.

> Right from the beginning, we realized to succeed we would need to build a really strong consumer brand with multiple touch-points. When you have some people who only decorate a room every 5 to 7 years, it's going to be exceptionally hard to build a strong enough brand that people will keep coming back. Our way around this, as well as selling multiple products, is to build a community and create content to make sure that people are consistently engaging with the brand, even if they are not purchasing the product. The other great thing we are finding is that the younger demographic decorates their home much more frequently. They are also looking to personalize more than ever before. We want to inspire our customers weekly so that when they are ready to make a change, we are their first thought. When a strong brand is combined with being able to get everything you need and an unbelievable customer experience, we think we can create something special.

Multiproduct, omnichannel, multiple geographies

As well as having a dynamite brand, the other thing which stands Lick apart is the scale of their ambition. It's not just multiple products. They also aim to be both omnichannel and international as quickly as possible. Omnichannel enables Lick to access a broader customer base and helps further build the brand. Their first steps into retail will be in a partnership with the online furniture retailer MADE.

> We have been approached by a number of retailers, but we believed MADE was the best fit. It is a great opportunity to build trust with the product and brand. In addition, MADE have strong exposure across Europe, which can also unlock a lot of value.

Explaining their international objectives, Lucas went on.

> At the moment, we only have fulfilment from the UK, which means the
> shipping is expensive and slow to get to mainland Europe. We want
> the customer experience to be the same for an international customer
> as a domestic one. To enable this, we will be creating fulfilment hubs
> in local markets from next year to make sure we can offer the same
> user experience in multiple markets. We have also built the platform to
> incorporate multi-language and multi-currency. We are ready for this
> to be turned on tomorrow. The key step, before we flip the switch, is
> establishing the fulfilment centres.

The Lick vision is a comprehensive illustration of launching a modern
DTC company. It is multi-product, multi-channel, multi-region, caters
for individual households as well as trade customers, with it all
wrapped up in a super slick brand to do the selling.

Money talks

Unsurprisingly, to have all this, it has required some serious venture
capital (VC) backing (Lick have recently raised £3 million in addition
to a sizeable pre-seed round). Without the scale of their ambition, it
is unlikely that Lucas and Sam would have secured the funds needed
to establish the business. Lucas explains:

> The VC world now has the scars of too many unprofitable DTC
> companies. While they appreciate the direct relationship, to get their
> backing, we had to show them this was not just about the old model
> of a DTC, which required lots of money to be spent on customer
> acquisition. The execution of the brand, the multiple vertical and
> omnichannel approach, made them realize we had much better
> foundations than the older iterations of DTC businesses. The thing we
> did well was to raise a good amount of seed capital to establish our
> brand and verticals [sales channels and product types], which in turn
> has allowed us to do further successful raises.

Introducing Clearing and a new way to treat pain

When meeting the founders who contributed to this book, I imagined that the £3–4 million for a seed round that Lick received was at the top end of what a modern DTC brand might raise to get started. But then I was introduced to Avi Dorfman, founder and CEO of the digital pain relief platform, Clearing.

Avi's journey with pain relief began when he stepped in to help a loved one who, like millions of other Americans, was suffering from a battle with chronic pain. Avi described years of going from doctor to doctor until he was finally introduced to his now co-founder, Dr Jake (Jacob) Hascalovici. What made Jake different from the other physicians that Avi met was that he introduced himself as a pain doctor. Avi explained why this mattered:

> I had no idea pain doctors even existed. The problem is that they practise under the titles of neurologists and anaesthesiologists. If you are looking for a doctor to treat chronic pain, these specialists are not easy to find. As well as not being obvious who they are, there are also not enough of them. While up to 50 million Americans are dealing with pain, there are only 7000 doctors in pain management.

Not being able to find a specialist pain doctor is why millions of Americans would generally visit their family doctor for pain relief. The typical treatment is being given a prescription for pain killer drugs, many of which contain opioids. Opioids provide excellent short-term pain relief, but they come with some severe side effects. According to the National Institute on Drug Abuse, these side effects include addiction, drowsiness, confusion, euphoria, hypoxia and risk of death. Even more tragically, overdoses are a massive problem. A 2017 study from the US Department of Health stated that more than 115 people a day were dying from an opioid overdose.

Meeting Jake was a game changer for Avi. His loved one was out of pain within five months of treatment, and Avi recognized the vast need and opportunity for helping more people who were suffering. Avi and Jake started to discuss how they could find ways to combine Avi's technology and entrepreneurial skills with Jake's medical background to help others find and connect with doctors to get treatment for their pain. The pair kept talking, and when the COVID-19 pandemic hit in the spring of 2020, the solution revealed itself. With large amounts of the United States encouraged to stay at home, Jake found that most of his patients were no longer visiting his clinics and had moved to online platforms to access their medical care. Avi recalled:

> Jake told me his whole practice had changed, and he believed it would never be the same. Patients did not want to come in unless they needed an injection. Patients had moved to the cloud, and it made so much sense that this would be the future. We spent the next month or so finding out what it meant to diagnose and give treatments digitally. We saw a profound behaviour change and with it an opportunity for setting up a digital-based health care practice.

Things moved quickly from there. The concept was cemented in June 2020. By 9 July, they went out to raise $2 million of pre-seed capital, and by 29 July, they closed the round with $6 million of investment secured.

Avi and Jake had shown their investors how they can use qualified doctors to interact with patients digitally and prescribe treatments. The initial platform works like this; you fill in a detailed medical questionnaire, which is assessed by a qualified practitioner, who will then prescribe a personalized care plan including opioid-free prescription-strength medicine. Once the treatment plan has been prescribed, Clearing customers will receive their products monthly and also have the option to add on CBD remedies and nutraceuticals to their order. In addition to the physical products, Clearing also gives each customer a personalized exercise plan and access to clinical follow-ups.

Experiments and continuous learning

While the concept is strong, Clearing's success will depend on getting a deep understanding of what their customers need and learning how to best serve them. Figuring this out is the responsibility of Avi's co-founder Yakov Kagan, formerly a growth lead at ride-sharing taxi company Uber, the code learning platform Codecademy and fintech flexible payment company Bread. Yakov's job is finding out who a Clearing customer is and what they want. Who they are is not just a matter of demographics. It is also what Yakov calls 'psychographics'. Psychographics is more than just understanding age, gender location, education etc., it is also a study of consumers based on their activities, interests, values and opinions.

Yakov has used questionnaires, landing pages, surveys and thousands of interviews to determine who a Clearing customer is and how they think. After all these tests, they now understand their psychographic customer is matched to a 45- to 64-year-old female who is proactive about her health.

Knowing who your customer is and what they want is the cornerstone of brand building. Armed with this knowledge, Clearing turned to Red Antler to help them create a memorable brand. Over the past decade, Red Antler has become the go-to branding and design agency for dozens of the best DTC brands with a roster including Casper, All Birds, Snowe, Birchbox and Ursa Major. Clearing will need to communicate the benefits of using a new treatment and, importantly, build confidence that the treatment works and the company is trustworthy. To achieve this, the brand needs to be strong and impactful, which is why Avi and his team wanted to work with an agency like Red Antler, which has a proven track record of creating iconic disruptive brands. One of the first things Red Antler did was convince Avi that his original brand name of 'feelrelief' was not ownable enough. It took quite a few iterations, but when 'Clearing' was suggested, it just felt right. In her book, *Obsessed*, Red Antler co-founder Emily Haywood describes the essence of a brand being at its most powerful when it speaks to someone's sense of self. With its light and soothing name, Clearing described how its customers would 'feel' once they had interacted with it.

Launching smart

With the brand designed, products, services and processes defined, medical advisors on board and an operational team in place, Clearing launched in May 2021. It was not a big bang launch. Instead, the Clearing team favours a much more disciplined approach. Yakov took me through the thinking:

> We know there is a group of people who will be desperate for what we offer and will seek us out. After that, however, we need to find customers, and that is much harder to do. We could spend lots of money on advertising, but when you are still learning, it's an inefficient and wasteful use of money. You are better served spending less because you initially don't know what is going to work. If you go big pre-emptively, you are effectively guessing.

This seemed like sound advice; however, at the time of the interview, Clearing had just announced they had raised $20 million of seed round funding. Even with this money in the bank, Yakov dispelled any notion of a more gung-ho approach.

> It is true, with the investment, expectations are high. However, our investors are betting on us getting it right. For me, it means we are now able to do even more experiments by working with more agencies and contractors on everything from design to pricing, trial periods, advertising channels, brand messages and more.

The rigour demonstrated by contemporary DTC brands is in contrast to a few years ago when it was all about acquiring customers as quickly as possible with the hope that the LTV (lifetime value) of the acquired customer would eventually pay back all the upfront marketing costs.

The new rulebook

It is not that modern DTC brands don't spend money. They spend it differently and hopefully more wisely. The big difference is that today's DTC environment is much more mature, and consumer expectations are now much higher than they once were. What could pass for an MVP a few years ago would not gain today's consumer's attention or trust. The other big difference is the focus on accelerating profitability. Yakov told me, 'We are testing our product offering in one channel first and won't move on until we have proven success in that one customer acquisition channel. We focus on today and not success tomorrow. Solving today's problems will set us up for longer-term success.' Clearing's telehealth model could work for many more conditions and across many more geographies. However, for now, the team have a ruthless narrow focus on pain care relief for 45- to 65-year-old women living in the United States.

Having a very defined strategy is shared by both Lick and Clearing. For Lick, it is all about making the home decorating experience easy and enjoyable. For Clearing, it is about helping the millions of chronic sufferers access safe and effective treatment for their pain. Having a clear path to growth and demonstrating a track record in high growth businesses has also allowed both companies to access venture capital investment. Given how VCs are now aware of the limitations of DTC (high customer acquisition costs, lots of competition, lower barriers of entry, etc.), it is not easy to convince them you can overcome these issues. Even if you can succeed in getting funding, VC money brings more pressure on the founding team to make good on that investor faith. With more funding, the risks and rewards have been magnified. You are now playing a higher stakes game.

High pressure and high risk or not, both businesses have a firm belief it gives them the best chance. Lucas told me, 'If you create a consumer brand without capital, it's a really hard slog. If you go down that path, you are at risk of competitors coming in with more resources. It is also much harder to change the dynamics of the existing market.'

LESSONS FROM LICK AND CLEARING

1 Today's realities mean that if you are about to start a DTC business and what you offer is not completely revolutionary, you need an effective entry plan and the resources to execute it. Otherwise, you will be lost among the abundance of competition.

2 To make sure they can stand out (and also convince investors they are a credible investment), both Lick and Clearing put developing a strong brand identity as one of their first tasks. Some businesses will want to

see if their idea works and develop the brand over time. Lick and Clearing believe that success (and investors) will not be obtainable without a strong brand from the get-go.

3   By having a portfolio of products and services, Lick can attract more customers. Multiple offerings also allow them to see which ones gain the most traction. Clearing has a narrower portfolio but is continuously and systematically testing to figure out how best to serve its customers.

4   Both businesses have been successful at raising large amounts of money to execute their plans. But they are also both focused on not being wasteful with that cash. Lick is investing in the brand and product rather than just buying customers via digital advertisements. Clearing has a programme of doing thousands of tests where they invest a little to learn a lot. Then, once they have figured out what works, they remove the guesswork and know where to deploy their resources.

10

The importance of an emotional connection with your customers

tails.com

At Peppersmith, one of the things we did well was always making it easy for customers to get in touch. We weren't shy to publish our phone number and made sure our postal and email addresses were easy to find. The inspiration for this came from my time at innocent drinks. They were famous for their 'feeling bored? Pop round to Fruit Towers or call the bananaphone for a chat' messaging, and it sat proudly on their labels and website, complete with phone number and address. It was an open house, and everyone in that business was encouraged to pick up the phone and talk to anyone who got in touch. This openness resulted in excellent conversations with customers, journalists, random cold callers and everyone in-between. Although picking up the phone could be a bit of a distraction, it meant that the end customer was always front of mind. You would never tell a customer you didn't have time to answer their questions, and a bit of banter and making time to chat was not only encouraged but expected. Better still was the open-door policy for people to come and visit the office. You'd have thought that going to see a bunch of people tapping away on keyboards or sitting in a meeting room would be a dull day out – but it always amazed me, the pleasure and excitement you'd see on the faces of those visitors, who rocked up to see where the magic happened. We took this philosophy with us to Peppersmith and ensured we were always on hand to chat with our customers, providing them with the best customer service and engagement possible.

Coming from two forward-thinking consumer product businesses that encouraged customers to get in touch, I'm always surprised when I see organizations that don't adopt this policy. Depressingly, a lot of DTC companies are often guilty of being hard to reach. While writing this book, I found that still, some DTC companies don't make their phone numbers or addresses clear or easy to find. Sure, there's usually an email address and sometimes an AI-driven chatbot, but talking directly to another human is hard work. Although it's a slowly disappearing practice, many businesses still consider it okay to give out a generic email address or web form as the only method for getting in touch. As we will discover, this is a false economy and a risky strategy, especially for any new challenger brands.

Personalized dog food

James Davidson, the co-founder and CEO of tails.com, tells the most fantastic cautionary tale about why hiding behind your technology is the wrong approach and what magic can materialize when you welcome direct and candid dialogue into your business.

I met in person many of the people behind the businesses that you'll read about in this book: I relished the chance to check out their workspace. However, in the case of tails.com, I was a little reluctant. The reason being – dogs. And lots of them.

As the name suggests, tails.com is a pet food business focusing on dog food. What makes it stand out from conventional pet food businesses is that they recognize that every dog (and they mean every single one) is different. Its age, breed, health conditions, activity levels and individual taste preferences mean that an off-the-shelf bag of dog food will almost certainly leave it short of the optimal diet it needs to thrive. Getting this wrong leads to disease, behavioural issues and an unhappy pet. tails.com is all about optimizing the mix of the right ingredients in the right amounts to help make sure your dog lives a long and healthy life.

They really do love dogs too, which means, if you have one (and many who work there do), every day is a 'take your dog to work' day. I had the chance to hang out with Noodle the long-haired dachshund, Baloo the beagle, Elmo the Cavapoo and the rest of the gang. Although I am a dog fan, I have a dog allergy, which meant that I had to find somewhere less dog-friendly to meet with James unless I wanted to wheeze and sneeze my way through our interview.

Safely out of harm, James and I had a long chat about his business and spent much of that time talking about customer service and customer communication. At the very beginning, tails.com was one of those DTC businesses that made getting in touch tricky. But, James explained, 'not only is that a bad business decision generally – it was also something that nearly killed us before we even really got going'.

Assembling a formidable founding team

tails.com was founded in 2013 by Joe Inglis, the British television vet and author who had the initial idea and Graham Bosher (the same guy who had previously established graze.com). Graham used his networks to hand-select a co-founding team of eight, including James, to run the supply chain. It was a crack founding team. James had recently quit his role as head of supply chain at innocent drinks – yes, the company with the bananaphone. Graham had just stood down as CEO for graze and was ready to apply himself to another DTC project, and Joe was to be the expert product lead. As a vet, Joe saw a lot of unhealthy dogs and knew that having the wrong nutrition was one of the key reasons he was spending so much time caring for them.

It was this co-founding team who were tasked with developing Joe's concept of tailored dog food into a DTC business. It was a big co-founding team, but that was needed to match the ambitions of the business. The demanding USP was a product made specifically for each dog depending on its size, breed, age and characteristics. When I met James, he was keen that I mention the whole team to share the credit for cracking the concept. The team makeup was Joe, focused on product, Graham the initial CEO, and James headed up the supply chain. Steve Webster, Karen

Freeman and Mark Holland led the technical and software build with Kat Linger establishing the brand identity and Paul Cook figuring out growth marketing.

They set about crafting the business plan, designing the product and raising cash. Helped by his track record, Graham quickly raised the money needed to get the business going from a mix of friends, family and his network. Funding completed, the first major task was to build a factory capable of making individual meal plans for tens of thousands of dogs each week. One of the advantages of a DTC business is that it attracts technically minded people. The tails.com team were no exception, and this meant the concept of building a factory from scratch was going to be a whole lot of fun. The team set to work, intending to have the flexibility to make thousands of different meal plans each day, with the efficiency to allow a decent output and to keep costs low.

On arriving at this part of the story, James shared a perfect analogy from the film *The Founder* about how Ray Croc built the McDonald's empire. In the film, there's a scene where Ray Croc and the original two McDonald brothers are designing the perfect layout for a fast-food kitchen. Ray and the brothers draw out the kitchen in chalk on the ground and configure it repeatedly until they find the optimum layout. It's hard to know how much artistic licence is in this scene, but James told me that this is precisely what he and Graham did to ensure the best possible design and process for the tails.com factory. Having spent many hours on their plans, they knew what size factory they would need and found the ideal space under the Heathrow airport flight path in West London. 'Doing this level of planning upfront meant we priced our products properly.' James explained:

> We knew exactly how much everything would cost to make, so we knew what we had to charge to get a workable margin. We designed a system that was efficient enough for us to be competitive. We made sure we got many things right from the very start – not only the factory but also key supplier relationships. I'm glad we did this as it saved us a lot of pain later down the track.

With money secured, the factory set up, the website designed and the team in place, James and the rest of the team were ready to launch. In July 2014, the website went live, production started and the marketing team began to spread the word. tails.com was open for business.

Building a fail-proof business and then nearly failing

Given the team's size, experience, meticulous preparation, a big market with an observable demand, an innovative product, highly competitive pricing, money in the bank and a purpose-built factory, how could they possibly fail? The lesson in this story is that they very nearly did. For all their experience, research and preparation, their Achilles' heel was that they didn't fully understand what their customers wanted from them, and this misunderstanding nearly cost them everything.

Alarm bells started to ring only shortly after the launch. The numbers didn't look good – their customer acquisition costs (CAC) were high, and their customers' projected lifetime value (LTV) was low. Simply put, the money they needed to spend to get a customer far outstripped the predicted profits each customer would make. The numbers told them it wasn't going to be a profitable business. The initial conclusion was that there weren't enough people willing to buy pet food in this way. James summed up the problem, 'We had an amazing product, but no one actually wanted it.'

It looked bad, and the numbers were saying this venture would fail, all the investors would lose their money and the team would be out of a job. For Graham it was the predicament of the investors that weighed heavily. Many of the investors were friends, family and close personal contacts, and Graham felt a huge weight of responsibility towards them. He realized they could potentially lose everything and had concluded that it might be best for them to cut their losses, shut down the business and return any cash that remained.

So less than six months after launch, Graham convened an emergency shareholders meeting to discuss the idea of closing the business. Fortunately, James and the other co-founders still believed in the business despite what the raw data was telling them. While there were certainly issues, they had only just started and were convinced they could make things work. James stood up after Graham had presented the option to shut shop and made an impassioned alternative pitch to continue. As the COO (essentially third in command) and being new to DTC, James wasn't sure how his proposal to carry on would be received. After an intense discussion, the investors agreed that the business should continue and try and turn the numbers around. The investors were supportive and encouraging of James' conviction. It was also agreed that James would now lead the company and prove it could work. James was now the CEO.

James recalled:

> The afternoon after the meeting, I went back into the factory, told the team what was going on and did my best Churchillian speech, asking everyone the question of what they wanted to do. Did they want to go home, or did they want to fight to keep this thing alive? To my relief, everyone was like, no way, of course, we're still all-in.

So, with the team rallied, the next task was to figure out the problems and find some fast fixes.

The turnaround

The first thing they did was turn off the marketing taps to buy themselves some time while working out what was going wrong. The first job was to solve their acquisition and retention problems. To do this, they needed to talk to their customers to find out what was stopping them from either signing up or, if they did, continuing with the service. The first clue was that, up until this point, talking to customers was quite hard to do. At that time, tails.com was a very transactional business. You signed up, probably for a free trial bag, and got your dog food. Then silence. 'Email notifications were kept to a minimum, no follow-ups were made and reaching our customer service team was somewhat painful,' explained James. 'At the time, this was how a technology-driven DTC business did its thing. It was expected that you should have an automated experience with minimal touchpoints.' While this may have been a good model for a tech business, the team had badly misunderstood their customers' needs and expectations in the domain of animal lovers.

James and his team, intuitively knew the answer would come from prioritizing customer service and feedback. To enable this, they increased the size of the customer service team, put a phone number on the website and started to engage with customers personally. Only once tails.com began engaging directly with their customers, did they understand what they needed to do.

A few critical things quickly came to light.

There was an error in the algorithm, which resulted in sending a bunch of dogs too much food. This error made some of our customers think we were trying to rip them off. We were also not emailing customers when their next delivery would arrive, leaving them confused and anxious. The website was also quite hard to navigate. It was a UX [user experience] issue, which we would not have been able to solve with data alone.

Fixing these problems resulted in a rapid increase in both converting customers and retaining subscriptions.

The most profound thing that happened once we opened ourselves up was the realization that most people wanted to contact us to ask questions about the well-being of their dog. It wasn't only about pricing or deliveries; many of the calls were about how best to care for their pet. We needed to build more trust, and to do this, it meant spending our time talking with our customers. It wasn't just talking to them and helping them with their animals that helped us build trust. We also did simple things like making sure it was super easy and obvious how to cancel a subscription. This was seen as quite radical in the mid-2010s. As you don't want people to unsubscribe, so it's risky to make it too easy. We wanted to show we weren't some faceless company just in it for the money. We needed to build more trust in any way we could.

The other thing that happened was we started getting increasingly positive feedback about what was happening to the dogs we were feeding. Messages like; 'thank you for helping my dog jump over stiles again', 'this is the first time in years my dog is playing with his ball' or 'thanks for giving my dog her life back'.

It was after a long and emotional call from a customer, explaining how tails had transformed their dog from a seriously ill and lethargic animal into an energetic bundle of joy, did it dawn on James that the business shouldn't simply be treated just as an opportunity to do DTC in pet food. It needed to have a bigger purpose: helping dogs have the happiest, healthiest, longest lives possible.

Opening up

They stopped being a guarded, transactional business and became more open, communicative, helpful and supportive. With this new attitude, the company quickly started to build customer trust and credibility. Credibility was the key to driving acquisition, and trust drove loyalty.

It worked. The numbers turned around, customer acquisition costs declined, and more and more customers signed up. What's more, they ended up sticking around well beyond the three years the team had allowed in their business planning. Of course, the team didn't necessarily think that their customers would stop using them after three years; it was just the limit they had set themselves to make sure their LTV calculations weren't overly optimistic.

In fact, at the time of writing, tails.com is a rapidly expanding business with more than 300 staff and 260,000 customers. Thirty thousand reviews and a 5-star rating on Trustpilot tell you their customers appreciate their efforts. The rest of the category has also taken notice and just over four years from launch, the company sold a majority stake to Purina, Nestlé's pet food arm. This investment enables tails.com to expand globally and expand into other pet food categories. James and his team were right to believe they could get it right.

Looking back, James said that they fell into the trap of an over-reliance on data and analytics.

I think that, like many people in DTC or any business based on technology, you end up spending a lot of time geeking out over the data. When you do this, you forget that for all the correlations and clever stuff the numbers can spit out, this is only part of the picture. You need to really understand why customers are doing what they're doing and not just rely on the numbers. You need to speak to customers directly, and then compare what they say to what the numbers are telling you. The other thing you need to give yourself is time. When we started, we had a monthly subscription schedule, so when it came to customer behaviour, it took a long time for an accurate picture to emerge. If you see the first few data points on a curve and extrapolate, you can produce a pretty terrifying-looking curve. You need more data points to really understand what direction you're heading in, and that takes time.

LESSONS FROM TAILS.COM

1   Understand what your customers want. To do this, you need to talk to them, not just look at the data. Numbers alone won't tell you how your customers feel about you.

2   Have a purpose and build trust. Serving customers should not be purely transactional. Customers need to know you care, and you have to understand what they need from you.

3   Give yourself time to understand what's happening. To do this, you may need to be conservative on things like marketing spend in the early days. While you may be confident, it is prudent to give yourself time to fix any issues before you exhaust your seed capital. Even the most carefully planned operation will still have things it needs to correct.

4   If things look bad at the beginning, don't give up. Instead, give it your best shot at making the business work. Then, even if you fail, you won't have any regrets or the wonder of what could have been.

5   Use your investors as a sounding board. Not being in the trenches means they will have a different perspective. So get their advice and make sure you have their support. tails.com wouldn't have survived if their shareholders hadn't believed in the business when the going got tough.

11

From startup to IPO. How Casper achieved unicorn status but has still to win over Wall Street

Casper

History makers

When the story of the DTC revolution is written in 50 years, one of the companies sure to be in that account will be the mattress company Casper. In seven short years since they launched, they have become a catchall for everything good and bad about DTC companies. When you hear the name Casper, you likely know what the company does; however, due to everything that has been said, it can be hard to work out if they have been a success or not. Earlier in the book, Casper and the mattress industry has been mentioned as an example of a DTC category where brands have to invest so much money into customer acquisition that none of them can ever turn a profit. Could this be true, and if so, how did Casper achieve unicorn status (valued at over $1 billion) shortly before listing on the Nasdaq stock exchange? To talk me through the highs and lows of the journey was product lead and co-founder Jeff Chapin. Jeff was part of a five-person founding team, a big team for a business with a big ambition.

The founding team

Unlike the rest of the founding team, Jeff was a few years older and, before joining, had spent the previous ten years at legendary product innovation company IDEO. Jeff was a consultant working on every-thing from consumer goods, pharmaceuticals, aerospace projects and pro-bono assignments, including sanitation projects in Cambodia, East Timor, Kenya, Nigeria and Vietnam. It was hard graft but fulfilling work with the bonus of Jeff meeting his now-wife who was also work-ing in Cambodia. It was his wife who introduced Jeff to his soon-to-be Casper co-founder Neil Parikh who was her classmate at Brown medi-cal school. Though Neil eventually dropped out of medical school, he and Jeff remained friends. The Casper story started in 2013 when Neil joined an incubator programme to create a new business with fellow Brown University alumni Luke Sherwin and Gabe Flatman. It was at the incubator that they met the more seasoned entrepreneur Philip Krim and the idea of a DTC mattress business was first discussed. Phil, Neil, Luke, Gabe and Jeff would be the founding team of Casper, but of all the products or services in the world, why did they choose mattresses? For one, the business of sleep was not new to them. Phil had previously founded a series of dropshipping e-commerce mattress businesses, including AngelBeds.com and SleepBetterStore.com. Neil's dad was a sleep doctor, and Neil knew that Jeff had previously worked on mattress industry projects at IDEO. With this insider knowledge, the team knew a thing or two about the mattress industry, and there was a lot they did not like about it.

Jeff told me:

> It was a huge industry with a few companies making huge gross margins, and candidly it was about as unsexy industry you could get. The pricing was opaque, and the brands were boring and unfriendly. The whole experience of visiting a strip mall store and being pressured by a commission salesperson to buy a mattress you knew nothing about other than lying on it for 5 minutes was lousy. There was a lot of consumer confusion, and the retail experience was horrific. We cottoned onto this perfect opportunity where prices were overinflated, and consumers had to make big purchasing decisions on a product they would use for the next ten years with very little information.

The Casper pitch was the classic DTC distribution solution. Casper would offer a better-quality product at a better price delivered directly to your door. Furthermore, to remove the consumer risk of buying the wrong product, they would offer a 100-day money-back guarantee and a ten-year warranty on your mattress.

Turning around sceptical investors

Initially, the idea was not well received by potential investors. They did not like the industry; as Jeff mentioned, it was very uncool. They only had one product. The buying frequency was low. There were also fears that consumers needed to touch the product before they bought it. The team had to grow a thick skin as the rejections came thick and fast. This was until they were introduced to Thrillist founder and VC Ben Lerer. Lerer was already an early evangelist and believer in the DTC model, having already invested in Warby Parker.

Furthermore, Lerer had also identified the mattress space as ripe for disruption and was already looking at DTC mattress models. When they were introduced, the stars aligned, and they were a perfect fit for each other. Lerer Ventures signed up and became their lead investor for initial seed rounds. Once they had Lerer on board, they suddenly had credibility, and other prominent investors such as Northwest Venture partners also joined the round. With Ben's backing, they went from being a business nobody believed in to being oversubscribed and raising just under $2 million to fund the fledgling business.

The investment allowed them to start work on developing their brand identity. To do this, Casper became an early client for DTC branding agency Red Antler. In the meantime, Jeff built a little lab in Rhode Island to develop, test and iterate on the perfect mattress. They tested their prototypes on friends and family to work out the optimum mix of comfort and support. One of these early testers was now head of brand Luke's German flatmate Kasper. At 6 feet 6 inches, Kasper was not a great guinea pig as he was too big for just about any test mattress he was asked to try. Kasper proved to be a regular source of feedback and amusement and it was he who provided the genus of the brand name.

The joy and pain of hitting your annual sales target in 60 days

The business launched in April 2014 with initial sales projections of $1.8 million in the first year. Very quickly more and more people were turning their heads. It took only 60 days to reach their year one target, and by the end of 2015, they had annual sales of over £100 million. One of the things that allowed such stratospheric growth was that they had a negative cash conversion cycle. This meant that customers paid for stock before the business had to pay their suppliers. However, growing this quickly was not without its difficulties. With the supply chain playing catch up, customers had to wait longer than advertised, which meant lots of customer service calls to apologize and explain the delay. To keep customers happy, the team resorted to buying airbeds from Amazon and sending them to any customer who was now sleeping on the floor due to the backlog.

The thesis about the mattress industry being ripe for a disruptive DTC model was proving correct. What's more, the brand was a hit and consumers loved the novelty of receiving a mattress in a Casper box (the mattress was compressed and folded into a golf bag sized rectangular cardboard box for easy transportation and delivery). YouTube was all of a sudden full of videos of people sharing their unpacking experience of their Casper mattress, filming the strange satisfaction of it reshaping itself once free from its boxy prison.

With its initial success under their belt, the team were hungry for more and so were their investors. Even with sales of $100 million, there was plenty of headroom for growth, with the US mattress industry totalling around annual sales of $18 billion. As well as launching their mattress into other geographies, Casper also wanted to be known as a sleep business going beyond mattresses into other products and services to help you get a better night's sleep. 'Investors were flocking to us, and every round was oversubscribed, and we were getting these huge valuations. It was eye-popping. We thought this is not much dilution for a lot of money.' As the business continued to grow, the investors kept backing the team. A 2014 Series A round of $13.1 million was swiftly followed by a Series B in 2015 ($55 million), a Series C in 2017 ($170 million) and finally a Series D in 2019 of a further $100 million. Investors included follow-ups from initial investors including Lerer Hippeau, strategic corporate investors such as Target and a host of PR friendly celebrity backers including Ashton Kutcher, Nas, Tobey Maguire, Leonardo DiCaprio and Adam Levine.

Casper raised a lot of cash. It turned out they were going to need this money, but not for the reasons they first thought.

175 is a crowd

By the mid to late 2010s, Casper was no longer the only show in town when it came to online mattress companies. The conditions that made Casper such an initial success attracted a host of competition to enter the market. In the United States, Purple, Leesa, Nectar, Tuft & Needle and in the UK, Eve, Emma and Simba were now all playing the DTC card. They were attracted to the category because they could utilize the same financing and supply chain advantages as Casper. As fast followers, they also benefited from how Casper had legitimized and established the trend of buying a mattress online.

The influx of competition made Casper determined to double down: 'Because we saw a bunch of copycats coming up. We were in a rush to become a global brand. We wanted to be the first major entrant in Europe.' So the company that established first-mover advantage in the United States was now in an arms race both home and abroad.

As previously explained in the Lick story, all this competition gave consumers more choices and pushed up the customer acquisition costs of every company in this space. According to Jeff, the initial return on advertising spend was tremendous. 'One of the reasons investors poured so much money in was for every $1 we spent on Facebook we were getting $7 or $8 in revenue out. But that was back in 2015, and it's come down dramatically since then.' Casper found they soon had to spend much of their investors' money trying to outbid their competition. The battle was fierce and long. Jeff summed up the maths, 'If you have five competitors with $10 million to spend, we could easily outlast them, but if you have 100 competitors each with $5 million, then you are going to have to spend a tonne of money.' In 2019 mattress review site Goodbed.com estimated there were around 175 bed-in-box companies in the United States alone.

As digital advertising became cluttered and expensive, Casper turned to more traditional advertising space and had some success with some memorable subway adverts. However, just like online, these offline locations were too soon also coveted by the ever-increasing army of copycat brands. The heat was on. Just how hard Casper had to go to protect themselves against the increasing might of the competition is illustrated when they took three mattress review websites to court. The argument was that they were unfairly discriminating against Casper by giving them poor reviews compared to some of the other brands who had paid the websites for their favourable scores without declaring this practice.

Finding new ways to stay ahead

With online sales becoming more costly, Casper's next step was to open its own retail stores. These would include flagship stores in New York and San Francisco and a dozen smaller stores spread across the country. The challenge with retail stores is that it is a very different business model to the initial DTC business. As well as having to pay for space, staff and outfitting, the stores also need to carry inventory, which has a very different financial impact compared to the favourable cash flow process of their DTC model. Furthermore, Casper is the type of company that prides itself on great customer service, which meant they would often go the extra mile and pay for a taxi home for customers who had purchased a mattress. Of course, the mattress was still folded in the iconic Casper box, which magically fitted in the trunk.

Over in Europe, the company was also finding the mattress industry was very different to the United States. Jeff explained:

> In Germany, the [retail] mattress salesperson is a lot more trusted. To the point, you would let the salesperson touch your body and measure

your spine. No way would that happen in the US. Whereas in the UK, it was a race to the bottom. There were a bunch of companies selling very cheap mattresses, and we found we could not compete on price.

It was proving expensive and complicated to trade in Europe, especially as you also needed local manufacturing to be able to, cost-effectively, serve these markets.

To keep ahead, the final piece of the puzzle was for Casper to enter the traditional wholesale trade. This also proved a steep learning curve. Jeff explained:

> Initially, we didn't have any mattress insiders, and we did not know how to play the wholesale game. It was only once we hired an experienced salesperson who showed us how to create our displays in the store, build relationships by doing simple things like bringing a box of doughnuts and becoming friends with the salesperson did we move from being stuck in the dirty corner of the store.

The team also had to figure out new pricing and margin structures for their products, which is hard to do if you have built your business and pricing around DTC and not previously considered an omnichannel model.

'Don't buy Casper'

Though they were now in a demanding environment, the efforts made by Casper continued to grow the business. Their revenues grew from $250 million in 2017 to over $400 million by the end of 2019. Investing hard to grow your business and capture market share is hardly a rare strategy for many high growth startups and challenger brands. However, it's an aggressive approach and comes at a cost. Investing all your money in growth means that the enterprise will eventually run out of cash unless you find a way to reach profitability. The sustainability of the financial health of DTC businesses has come under more and more scrutiny in recent years, with many doubting the wisdom of the enormous valuations many VCs were happy to accept as they joined the DTC party. The suspicion around financial viability turned to scrutiny and scorn when at the start of 2020, Casper announced its intention to list on the stock exchange via an IPO. An IPO stands for initial public offering, which means rather than raising money via private investors, they would create shares to be sold on the New York Stock Exchange.

When you announce your intention to list your company publicly, one of your critical tasks is to produce a prospectus detailing your suitability and attractiveness for public investment in the form of an S-1 disclosure. One of the significant differences between selling shares on the stock exchange rather than to private investors is that you have to declare your current and predicted financial health to anyone who wants to see it. So for the first time, crucial financial details such as total revenue, gross margins, overheads and, importantly, profits (or in Casper's case, losses) were open to general scrutiny. Unfortunately for Casper, Wall Street analysts and financial commentators were not impressed with what they learnt. There were two main criticisms behind the collective negative sentiment. First, the IPO share price was lower than at the last private investment round less than a year before. This meant those later stage investors would lose money if they sold their shares at the launch share price. Second, the profit line was getting worse, not better over time, coupled with a slower growth rate. The lack of positivity around the IPO was summed up in a headline piece in *Forbes* entitled, 'Don't Buy Casper, The Latest Money-Losing IPO' published the day before the the company went public.

Unfair criticism, business realities and what next

According to Jeff, much of this criticism was unfair and was primarily a result of bad timing. For one, it was one of the first high-profile listings since WeWork's aborted attempted to go public in 2019. Like Casper, WeWork had put growth ahead of profitability. But, unlike Casper, WeWork's numbers were so skewed that they pulled out the listing after Wall Street declared them all but uninvestable.

The WeWork fiasco was the reason behind the *Forbes* headline as the financial markets had become wary of bailing out private investors of quick growth startups with public money. Most of all, however, Jeff's rationale for the lack of profit was due to the push to stay ahead. At the time of the IPO, Casper had been investing heavily into the roll-out of more retail sites, which have a longer payback cycle. In addition, they were getting a foothold in the wholesale market and were also in the process of winding down their expensive European operations.

Jeff stepped away from his operational role last year but is still a shareholder and a believer. While the share price still has a long way to get the value back to a pre-IPO unicorn level, the business continues to grow with a 2021 earnings call revenue prediction of around $600 million for the year, a 20 per cent increase on $485 million for 2020. At the time of writing, unfortunately, profitability, while improving, is still in the red. Jeff was honest about the criticism of the bottom line, '[In the years leading up to the IPO] We were on a treadmill running faster, faster, faster. This meant we were spending 95 per cent of our time racing and not looking at the business model. That is changing now, especially with the addition of the wholesale channel.'

After hearing the story first hand, it is difficult to be critical. Initially, the Casper team did a fantastic job of identifying and exploiting the mattress opportunity. They made a good product, worked hard to give their customers a great experience and developed a fantastic brand that really did make buying a mattress an appealing task. Then, things got tough for them because other businesses could quickly follow in their footsteps and use the same operating model to enter the market. The strategy of becoming the most prominent brand to differentiate and protect the business continues to pressure the bottom line. It has been hard for Casper to react to the speed and sheer volume of competition. Even as the trading environment got harder, they have been determined to stay the top dog in the category. First, they continued to look for ways to grow, including new products, international expansion, retail stores and eventually into wholesale. They also used the power of their brand, story and expectations of a bright future to raise lots of investment. The problem they had is they used this war chest more to out invest and outlast the competition rather than being able to use it to improve the fundamentals of the operating model. Time will tell to see if they can get the right balance between growth and financial suitability. If you believe they can continue to grow and also find a way to generate profits, now might be an excellent time to buy some shares.

LESSONS FROM CASPER

1 As one of the first high-profile DTC brands, Casper were able to show how a DTC model can usurp incumbent brands in what was a previously unsexy, opaque, customer-unfriendly category.

2 By finding a prominent investor who believed in the business rationale, they were then able to convince previously sceptical VCs that they would be a good investment. They were then able to double down on their investor appeal following exceptional early results and growth.

3 They focused on customer service and brand to get people excited about something as dull as purchasing a mattress. Buying airbeds for frustrated customers in the early days through to the craze of unboxing videos showed how well this worked.

4 Casper used their profile and impressive growth to attract investment. They have used this investment to stay ahead of the competition and protect their first-mover status. As well as investing heavily into marketing, new products and their European expansion, they have opened their own stores and recently begun to build a wholesale channel. Due to the sums of money spent, it will take time to tell if they have invested wisely; however, focusing on growth and market share allowed the company to continue to increase revenues, be attractive to investors and remain a leader in the category.

5 The business had the humility to backtrack on strategies that did not work out (e.g. transplanting the US brand and operating model into Europe). The reasons it did not work varied for different regions. For example, in the UK, they could not compete on price with the domestic competition. Whereas in Germany, the traditional mattress buying experience was more customer-friendly, and consumers were less willing to switch to a DTC model. Startup businesses have to try new things, but they also need to be flexible and humble enough to put the brakes on when it is clear the costs outweigh the benefits.

12

Using stress and burnout as the inspiration to build a better business

Heights

The first thing to know about Heights is that they have two founders with exceptional credentials. First up is Dan Murray-Setter, serial entrepreneur and host of top UK business podcast Secret Leaders. Since 2017 he has interviewed an impressive roster of founders from Hubspot, Brewdog, Allbirds, Deliveroo, Slack, Monzo and many more, including more than one founder featured in this book. His co-founder, Joel Freeman, is not as well known but equally impressive. Joel's first comment when we met was to apologize that the Heights logo on his t-shirt was not the correct shade of green to properly colour match the Heights brand Pantone. I wanted to get into the detail of what has made Heights one of the fastest growing and acclaimed DTC companies in the last couple of years. Joel and Dan granted my wish.

Not a supplement company

Heights' main product is a daily supplement; however, they do not describe themselves as a supplement company. Instead, Heights is a braincare company. Braincare is everything you need to keep your brain and mental well-being fit and healthy. According to Dan and

Joel, by regularly taking Heights supplements, you will benefit from increased energy and alertness, reduced anxiety, improved concentration and better sleep. Their claims are backed up by science with the products developed under the guidance of elite doctors and nutritionists. They also have an all-star cast of fans and contributors, including Stephen Fry, Alain de Botton, Dr Rangan Chatterjee and Michael Acton-Smith. Launching in January 2020, the company has just reached £2 million ARR (annual recurring revenue) and is reaching new 'heights' every month. The company and its founders are in a good place; however, this has not always been the case.

A flawed business model

Their adventure started in 2013 when the pair launched the mobile fashion app, Grabble. Grabble was an app that automatically curated a directory of all that was trending in the fashion world and allowed users to browse and buy products from up to 1500 brands and retailers, including Asos, Marks & Spencer, Harvey Nichols and Selfridges. Grabble proved to be a successful and popular app. Unfortunately, the business model did not work. As explained by Dan:

> The business was highly flawed as the technology was not quite there.
> At times it felt like we were holding things together with string and
> tape. And the middleman margins were also small. It meant with
> a heavily eroded margin, we basically imploded. We had too many
> problems to solve. Things were fine when things were starting to go well
> [a good number of app users]. And not fine when things were going
> really well [too many users].

The overheads needed to manage the technology meant the more products, retailers and users the app had, the more money it lost.

They had spent nearly five years growing the app and trying to figure out how to make a return from it. Despite its popularity, they eventually conceded they could not get the business model to work. Although they still had money in the bank, with no prospect of turning their finances around, they went back to their investors to tell them they should close the app. Rather than taking back what remained of the money in the bank, their investors suggested an alternative plan. Dan explained:

> We went to let them know we tried, but we failed. It's not worked. We suggested they should take their money back as we can't make this work. Their response was, rather than shutting us down, why don't we take the money we had left, keep it and have another roll of the dice.

Once they paid off their debts and ensured their team had decent severance packages, they had about £500,000 left. What remained was to be their pre-seed capital into a new venture. While it may seem like Dan and Joel had a free hit, the offer was not free of conditions. Their investors gave them three months to develop a new idea, and if they did not like anything presented, they would liquidate the business and take the money back.

The obstacle is the way

Closing Grabble and being given a deadline to come up with something new unsurprisingly took a toll on the pair. However, it was out of this hardship that redemption came. Both guys were finding things hard and suffering different stress-related ailments. Joel had stomach issues, and Dan was debilitated with chronic insomnia.

> I went six months without being able to sleep. I was completely incapacitated. Things were culminating with Grabble, and I was having anxiety, panic attacks, hot and cold sweats, the lot. I tried all the traditional therapies, including sleeping pills, but nothing really worked. It was only when a friend suggested I see a dietitian did I find a solution. I was very sceptical, but the dietitian diagnosed my problem and offered me a solution within about one minute.

Dan had been prescribed a course of supplements of omega 3, blueberry extract and vitamin B complex. It was not cheap, one month's supply cost Dan around £120, but it was worth it. 'Within a week, I was sleeping like a baby and gone from a supplement sceptic to a convert,' Dan told me. Dan had learned that good nutrition was needed to look after his mental health properly. He also discovered that while the science is quite well known, the brain health nutrition market was sorely undeveloped. The last important discovery was that the existing supplement market was not to be trusted. Dan and Joel found out the reason supplements have the common perception of being largely ineffective. The problem was that while the label can claim a benefit, in most cases, what happens is that to keep costs down, the quantities of ingredients are often about a tenth of the level they need to have any effect. 'The learning for us was this was a cowboy market, where the ability to rip people off is so blatant. These companies were preying on the fact that unless you were a nutritionist, you would never know. It is ridiculous.'

Trust as the foundation

The boys had their new idea: a brain health company that sold supplements that could be scientifically proven to have an effect.

> Before we even came up with the company name and product,
> we knew we wanted to be a company that could be trusted. Trust
> is our core value. For our product strategy, we only use trusted
> ingredients and make sure we are properly communicating the scientific
> benefit. We don't rely on allowed claims. We want to be backed up
> by science. For example, we could put a bit of magnesium into the
> capsules, which we could claim to aid sleep. However, we don't do this
> as we know we cannot fit an effective dose into our capsules.

It was the end of 2018. They had £500k in the bank, Grabble was in the past, and their investors were happy to continue to support them. Joel and Dan were ready to develop the best braincare supplement they could make. To do this, they teamed up with neuroscientist Dr Tara Swart and dietitian Sophie Medlin and set to work on the product. In the meantime, they also needed to start to build trust, and awareness of their mission. Dan continued, 'While Joel was heavily involved with product development, I was tasked with starting to develop a market and build trust. Trust is like a moat. It needs to be built drop by drop. It takes forever, so we thought we better start now.' The first 'product' the pair launched was a weekly newsletter called *Dawn* that shared the best and most accessible titbits of advice and braincare knowledge they could find. *Dawn* launched at the start of 2019, and over the following 12 months, the newsletter amassed more than 10,000 subscribers. The *Dawn* subscribers would eventually evolve into the founding members of the Heights community and provided the insight to help work out what stories, advice, products, and services were most helpful.

Trialling the products and getting support from a famous ally

By the end of 2019, Joel, with the help from Swart and Medlin, had the Heights braincare supplement ready to go. Before they officially launched, they wanted to make sure it worked and was a good consumer experience. So they turned to the newsletter subscribers, and from this list, they found about 200 people who agreed to become trialists. The idea was for them to trial the products for three months, and then if they liked it, they would be issued pre-launch codes to sign up for a regular subscription. When the service launched in January 2020, the company received £30,000 of orders in that first month. This level of interest meant there was not enough pre-order codes or stock to go around. It meant that unless you had a code and had quickly signed up, you were going to have to wait for new stock to be produced. One of the trialists who missed out on his chance to reorder was British comedian and actor Stephen Fry.

> It was very lucky, it could have been anyone else, and it would not have been the same story. Stephen had been a trialist and emailed in saying how much benefit he was getting from the products. His trial supply was now out, and he wanted to find out how he could continue. I promised to send him stock if he could say something nice about us for our website.

It was 6 January, just days after launch, and they were now able to put a ringing endorsement from Stephen Fry on their home page. Besides providing value due to his celebrity, Fry's endorsement added even more credibility as he had been very open about his mental health challenges in recent years.

Not being about how many pills are sold

The new business was up and running, and sales were going well, but Joel explained it was just the beginning and the mission went way beyond the supplements.

> We promote ten different pillars of braincare advice, with only one being nutrition. We see our job as building a community and knowledge around the braincare movement. Our community tells us which problems to solve, and we aim to put together all-star multidisciplinary teams to tackle these issues. This means that in the future, we could have digital products to help build habits in addition to more physical ones. We are open-minded about that. Rather than focusing on how many pills we will sell, we are outcome orientated, so we will do all we can for the best customer outcomes.

A content and community business

The broad focus on a braincare platform is why in addition to promoting the products and their benefits, Heights also spend a lot of time building and interacting with their community across different mediums. They have continued with the weekly newsletter, now called the *Sunday Supplement*, have a number one ranking health podcast called *Braincare* and a weekly braincare club on the Clubhouse platform, which has over 60,000 subscribers. Doing all this activity is intense, but it's how the brand acquires customers and retains them through the community it creates and the value they build. Dan told me:

> When we started out, our message was all about the science, but now we are more established it is much more about the community. As a subscription business, we need to keep our customers engaged years into their subscription, not just at the start. Content and community are the best ways to build and retain customers. This is our focus as a team far more than any kind of paid or acquisition marketing.

The success of their content and community intensive approach can be seen in the growth of subscribers (currently increasing at over 10 per cent per month) and phenomenal retention rates. 'Even though we make it easy as possible to change up and cancel your subscription, counter-intuitively, our retention is really good. It's about 90 to 95 per cent, which is insanely high,' explained Joel. The other thing Dan was also keen to highlight was that 'as a subscription business, our customers are not only paying for our products but buying a membership into a lifestyle where over the long term the benefits pay for themselves'.

Making things easy for their customers is a driving principle of the business. As well as making it easy to navigate their website, amend and cancel subscriptions, they appreciate that most of their community are busy people without lots of time to spare. For this reason, they design their weekly newsletters so you can read them in three minutes and their *Braincare* podcast episodes are only 15 minutes long. They also put exceptional effort into customer service.

In my experience, customer service is typically split between two types of contact. Either people got in touch to find more about the product itself (e.g. ingredients, benefits, packaging, etc.) or because they had an order issue (e.g. lost packages, change of address, payment query, etc.). Product expertise and looking after logistical issues requires two different skills. However, when I asked Joel how he approached these two different requirements, his answer was straightforward. 'I think it's easy. Find people who care about customers and also care about nutrition. We love talking to our customers, and they are always surprised by how much we care about their experience. We genuinely want to find out how we can make it better.'

Putting their community first fuels the growth of the business. Like some other brands in this book, they did a crowdfunding round and invited their pre-built community to participate. When the campaign was launched, they met their funding target in the first 20 minutes. Dan went on to write a widely shared article on LinkedIn detailing exactly how they were able to do this. It is titled 'How to raise £1M in 20 minutes in a record-breaking crowdfund'. Spoiler: it took a lot longer than the headline 20 minutes. In the post, Dan details each step of building a successful crowdfunding campaign from building crowdfunding into their Series A, choosing the right platform, leveraging their community and building excitement. If you are ever thinking of crowdfunding, it is something you should read.

The importance of making and controlling your margins

The community now is helping to develop new products by providing insights and feedback. Using these insights the next products to be released will be a probiotic supplement and a gratitude journal. Both will give additional ways to care for your mental well-being. A digital product is also in the works, but for now, the focus is on the best-in-class, scientifically proven, physical products supported by accessible, reliable and useful content. While Dan and Joel have extensive experience in digital products, they like physical ones because it is much easier to make and control their margins.

Dan reflected:

Our experience running Grabble made us very conscious of margin and very conscious that you don't have a business unless you have some reasonable margin to play with. You can't delight your customers unless you have a reasonable margin, and all of your avenues are completely cut off unless you have a business model that works. It was a very expensive lesson that we learned the hard way. We are now aware that every mistake we make, every time we need to make an apology, every bad Trustpilot review, every single thing that happens in your business eats away at your margin. Without a decent margin, we aren't going to be able to hire exceptional people, and without them, it's really hard to grow our business and surprise and delight our customers. The lesson was as we needed to make a good margin, we also needed to be conscious about the quality of our product and the communication of it. We need to make sure our customers respect the fact that it's a high-quality product, so we need to charge a fair amount for it.

LESSONS FROM HEIGHTS

1   By being honest with themselves and their investors about the flaws in their previous business, they earned the blessing of their investors to pivot into something new. Had they waited until they had entirely run out of cash, they would have found it much harder to start again.

2   They used their personal experience of stress and illness to identify a new category to develop. The critical insight was that while the science was there, the current products lacked trust. So they set out to solve this problem with better products and better communication.

3   In parallel to developing the product, they wasted no time building a community and developing trust and credibility via a weekly newsletter. The subscribers to this newsletter provided the first customers and have since evolved into the Heights community.

4   They create many touchpoints for their brand, including their website, newsletter, podcast and Clubhouse group. However, the one consistent thread is always to make any interaction as easy and useful as possible. Likewise, Heights's customer service is more than reactively dealing with issues and queries. Instead, they use this interaction to proactively find out more about their consumers and how they can serve them better.

5   From their previous business experience, they know that they must make enough margin on each sale to be able to properly serve their customers and grow their business. To do this, they ensure their customers understand what a fair price for their products is by communicating the provenance, quality and benefits of their ingredients and packaging.

13

How to use your low margin DTC channel as your omnichannel marketing machine

Ugly Drinks

Discussing George Orwell quotes and dystopian futures was a profound way to begin to describe your fizzy water brand and your mission. Classic Hugh Thomas. 'In a time of universal deceit, telling the truth is a revolutionary act' is attributed to Orwell when discussing his book *1984*. Whether he actually said it or not is uncertain, but in a time of fake news and mass marketing misinformation, it is a quote that resonates more than ever. Telling the truth when your industry is guilty of fuelling an obesity epidemic is why Ugly Drinks are beverage revolutionaries, and their mantra is 'The Ugly Truth'.

Ugly is a $10,000,000 international soda brand, started in the UK but now sell 90 per cent of their drinks in the United States. They are fiercely omnichannel, using DTC to recruit and educate customers and develop their business. At Peppersmith, we followed the playbook from our time at innocent drinks. If innocent launched today, it would likely follow the playbook of Ugly.

A thoroughly modern business

Ugly is different from most brands in this book because DTC only represents about 20 per cent of its revenues. The other 80 per cent is via retail and wholesale channels. Nevertheless, I felt compelled to tell the story because both in the United States and the UK, Ugly is held up as a brand that does DTC exceptionally well. Furthermore, the more I understood how they operate, I realized it is their DTC channel that powers their whole business.

Ugly is a thoroughly modern company. They have a small office in London and New York, which support a fully remote and globally distributed team across North America and Europe. Wherever they are based, the team's job is to build an international brand across multiple channels, using digital platforms and DTC as the primary way of recruiting, developing and informing. Leading the business is New York-based co-founder and CEO Hugh Thomas. Hugh had a lot to say about the soda industry and is on a mission to right some wrongs.

Loving the category

Hugh is a soda fanatic. As well as founding Ugly, he is an adviser, investor and cheerleader for multiple drinks companies. A quick look at his Twitter feed (@UglyHugh) features almost daily posts of his favourite products and packaging from drinks past and present. Hugh described why he is so passionate:

> I just fell in love with the beverage space, from my days as a Student Ambassador for Vitamin Water. There is something special about holding a can or a bottle and what it says about you and your identity. I also love the velocity and the rate of change in the category, which makes it so competitive.

After university, where in addition to promoting Vitamin Water Hugh gained a 1st in Management Science, he joined Heinz's graduate marketing programme. After a couple of years of corporate experience, Hugh was drawn back to the challenger space finding his way to US coconut water brand Vita Coco, which had just launched in the UK. Vita Coco was also where Hugh met his Ugly co-founder Joe Benn.

Vita Coco was the leading brand in the coconut water category that enjoyed explosive growth at the start of the last decade. The secret to the coconut water craze was its positioning as a healthier way to stay hydrated. Vita Coco is the clear water from coconuts and is high in electrolytes; however, it still had the same problem as most soft drinks. It contained a lot of sugar. Vita Coco was one of the healthier drinks on the market, with 11 g of sugar in each pack. For reference, a can of Coke contains about 35 g of sugar. But while there may have been less, the sugar was still there.

The problem with sugary drinks

It was the sugar issue that brought Hugh and Joe together as they knew first hand how much of a societal problem too much sugar had become. Hugh explains:

> At the time, my mum was a diabetic nurse, and Joe's sister was working at [the charity] Diabetes UK. I heard first hand how my mum's patients were trying to eat salads and cut out confectionery but still not losing weight. Their problem was that they were still drinking five or six cans of Coke a day. She explained that there was 35 to 40 g of sugar in a can. It is made worse because you consume it quickly, with no fibre, nothing to chew and nothing to digest. This means that as well as being high in calories, it hits your pancreas hard and spikes your insulin. I started doing my own research and found that here was this 90 billion dollar category with Coke and Pepsi getting rich from hundreds of millions of consumption occasions. While at the same time, in both the UK and US, over 30 per cent of all adults are now obese, and 60 per cent are overweight. Coke, Pepsi and the confectionery companies have had their own way for over 100 years and get away with things like sponsoring the Olympics. I get genuinely angry that Coca-Cola has an advertising tag line of 'Open Happiness' when their drinks are bringing distress to so many people.

So what do you do when you are a self-proclaimed beverage nut, with a mum who works as a diabetic nurse and a growing awareness of what sugary food and drinks are doing to the nation's health? 'We looked at the category and wondered if we could disrupt it with a drink that does not contain any of the bad stuff with a price point that was accessible to anyone whether you were living in Newcastle, London, Tennessee or in the Midwest.'

Starting out and choosing cans over bottles

Joe and Hugh quit Vita Coco in 2015 to bring their vision to life. The pair started experimenting, aiming to create a natural sugar-free alternative to mainstream soft drinks. They initially came up with a flavoured still water in a plastic bottle. Ultimately, this first product fell short. The main issue was a short and unstable shelf life. The shelf life issue made them look at cans, which preserved the drink much better. They also preferred the format as it was much more recyclable and allowed them to carbonate their drink. When this was all put together, they had their sweetener-free, sugar-free soda good enough to compete directly with a can of Coke or Pepsi. Or, as Hugh put it:

> We had a can of soda, we could wrap in a brand that does not tell people to be healthy. We would have no pictures of people doing Pilates and drinking green juice. No preaching about health. Just a product that's easy to switch to as it's a fun choice, refreshing and affordable.

If it seems strange that a drink with no sugar makes no health claims, Hugh explains why:

> We had this idea around us telling the truth and being transparent. We created a drink that has no sugar, no sweeteners, no calories and nothing artificial. There is no open for happiness, nor will give you wings or whatever. It's just plain sparkling water that is refreshing and hydrating. We had this idea about telling the ugly truth. We chose the name Ugly as it was counter-culture for the Instagram generation where you try and pretend to be beautiful, slim and aspirational. We are happy to be who we are.

A brand that stands out from the crowd
and celebrates being different

In addition to being happy to tell the truth about how bad regular sugary-laden soft drinks are for your health, Ugly is also pulling back the curtain on other areas where the drinks industry should be doing better. For every can of Ugly sold, the company donates to the charities Girl Up, which provides action on gender equality, and Oceanic Global, which help industry, global and local governments protect our oceans. The team identified these two issues as critical to the brand mission. Girl Up, as the drink industry remains very much male-dominated. And Oceanic Global, because Coca-Cola and Pepsico have been, time after time, recognized as the biggest contributors to the global plastic pollution problem. As with sugar, Ugly is comfortable calling out their much bigger rivals and choosing to take a different path.

Anyone who sees the brand on a can or interacts with the website will recognize the unique brand dynamic. The brand had to be strong and consistent with its identity, one that literally sticks its tongue out to the rest of the industry (the U on Ugly looks like a giant tongue, and each flavour has its own character, all with protruding tongues). The bold branding is intentional so the product can stand out on shelf. But, more importantly, Ugly is a digitally native brand designed to resonate on your computer and critically on your smartphone. When Ugly launched in London in 2016, it was obvious to Hugh and Joe that the internet would be their primary source for its marketing. Digitally native brands like Ugly focus on DTC for sales, at least initially and significantly use DTC to own the conversation and transaction between the brand and the end consumer.

Why DTC and omnichannel is consumer led

It's not that Ugly don't have retail customers; at launch, their main customers were the department store Selfridges and the seven Whole Foods Market shops located in London. While these prestigious outlets provided credibility, Hugh knew he could not build a scalable business that just relied on high-end London stores.

> When we launched, very quickly, we had tens of thousands of followers on Instagram from all over the country. Without our webshop, we would not have been able to serve hardly any of these people interested in our business. Being omnichannel was an obvious choice. We are a consumer-first company and will go and find the consumer wherever they are.

Due to the branding and on-point messaging, building a substantial social following came quickly. However, the company still had to figure out how to do DTC properly.

> We set up our DTC service from the same warehouse as our sampling. They had never shipped food and drink. At the time, they did mainly DVDs. So we had to learn the hard way; from how best to ship our drinks to how much it would cost and what do our customers expect in the way of customer service.

Managing high shipping costs

One of the biggest challenges for Ugly is what is known as value density. Value density is the value of the product relative to its weight and volume. Generally, the higher the value density, the cheaper it is to ship each unit. No such luck for canned soda where prices are low, and weight is high. The challenge of a low-value density product means shipping costs must be carefully managed.

As well as finding cost-effective warehouses and couriers, the way to mitigate these costs has been to make sure the order value is high enough to justify the shipping charge. Shipping costs mean it is not possible to offer single cans or packs of four. Instead, from the webshop, Ugly sell their products in cases of 24 for their regular 330 ml/12 oz cans or in boxes of 12s for their bigger cans, energy drinks and limited edition flavours. Even with larger shipments, margins are still tight; however, for Hugh, it's worth it. 'Although it is very hard to make decent margins DTC for a non-premium beverage company, it's how we get the word out, how we get people to buy into our dream and get people to discover us. For us, DTC is not a super profitable business model. Instead, it's a way to build a community and do things we would not be able to without DTC.'

Coming to America

The company spent the first couple of years incrementally improving their brand messaging and product experience. They also built a substantial retail presence gaining listings in mainstream supermarkets in the UK, such as Sainsbury's and Tesco. This progress was a good start, but if they were really going to make a dent in the market share of Coke, Pepsi and the like, they would have to do even more. They looked at expanding into Europe but were dissuaded by the complexity of lots of different languages and cultures to navigate. So instead, they decided to take on the drinks giants in their own backyard. In 2018, a little more than two years after launch, Hugh took a one-way flight to the USA to establish Ugly as a global brand.

From his HQ in Brooklyn, New York, Hugh told me:

> We are now a US business with a UK subsidiary. Being in the US is about building an international brand rather than a US or a UK one. We had to get used to different times zones, but we are a globally distributed team, managing DTC out of the UK with people in California, New York, Arizona and Tennessee to help us run our retail business. It was a big step, but we have always been very ambitious. One of the things I did that made a big difference was moving myself permanently and not trying to keep a foot in London. I had seen other British brands try and crack the US while from London and fail. I think it would have been impossible to do without me moving out here.

Using community engagement to drive innovation

The move has worked well, and you can now find Ugly in over 10,000 locations across the United States, including a nationwide listing with pharmacy chain CVS. Customer awareness and retention, however, is still very much built on a DTC base.

> We now have 100,000 on our DTC mailing list and 10,000 on our SMS service. From this, we can build our community. For example, we sent a survey out to our customers during the pandemic, asking them what flavours we should launch next. The response was insane, with over 40,000 replying. What was interesting was that nobody was asking for regular flavours like passion fruit or tangerine. Instead, they wanted marshmallow and other crazy flavours. This feedback made us realize what we needed to be different and provide a special experience. So we decided to use DTC to launch a new flavour each month and experiment with some more exciting choices. So now, if you are on our mailing list, we send you a message before we drop a new flavour inviting you to early access and a special price. What generally happens is most people take us up on the early invite, so by the time our limited editions are available to the public, they only last a few days.

As well as creating excitement amongst the Ugly fan community, the DTC limited edition program is the perfect testing ground for new products. In addition to analysing the sales data, a feedback survey is also sent to their customers to see how much they enjoyed the new flavour. Dr Ugly (the Ugly take on Dr Pepper), Marshmallow and Fruit Punch were hits. Pumpkin Spice, not so much. This feedback loop has resulted in turning some of the limited editions into permanent features in the range and extending their reach into Ugly's retail stockists.

> Our DTC supply chain is designed to be flexible, which allows us to add loads of value and feed our omnichannel strategy. It would take 6 to 12 months to work out whether a new product works in traditional retail. Using DTC, we can tell you in one week. Using DTC for innovation means everything we think of comes directly from the commitment of our community and our customers. It allows us to get as close to the customer as possible and enables them to tell us exactly what they want. DTC is more powerful than any research agency could ever be.

Keeping communication relevant

The limited editions are not the only way DTC precedes and fuels what happens in retail. Hugh explains:

> DTC helps our digital marketing capability enormously. For example, we can tell people when we are launching in a new Texan retailer. But it's no good just emailing everybody. If you live in New York, receiving a message about a new Texas location is irrelevant. What we can do is email our subset of Texan subscribers and let them know. Even then, we don't want to email everyone in Texas. We can even be more specific than that. For example, we might send a coupon for the people who live two miles away from the new store. If you are a little bit further away, we may send a targeted ad. We can also pinpoint local influencers who live within 5 miles of a location and get them to go into the store to take pictures. This blend of content, commerce and community is super powerful and drives all our sales channels.

Dealing with DTC low margins

Moving to the United States has helped Ugly broaden its customer base; however, it has further complicated shipping. Extreme temperature changes, the distances involved and increased touchpoints for each delivery mean that the shipping operations and costs are even more challenging to manage than in the UK. Again DTC data helps.

> We have used our customer data to optimize our delivery economics. We have worked out the best place to store and ship from in each region. We have worked hard to reduce proximity to our customers and the need for multiple warehouses. We now have sites in four or five locations across the country. Continually optimizing is essential as we have to operate with tight margins.

Even with low DTC margins, the company can prosper because only 20 per cent of revenue comes from DTC. Best of all, those DTC sales and customer interactions become the marketing bedrock that subsidizes the cost of building the more significant and more profitable retail business. 'The internet and social media democratizes commerce. We are a small brand that can now be spotted by somebody, wherever they are, and they can get a delivery the next day. Not only do we have an amazing marketing tool where anybody can find you, it also means you are in control of how you build your community and audience. This control means all our brand touchpoints – our ads, messaging, our website, all the way up to the unboxing experience. The reason I love SMS so much is that you really open yourself up. We create a two-way conversation, and that's where you get great engagement. I love talking to our customers even if they have a problem with the product. I love listening and learning, and if they have an issue, I love trying to turn them around and into advocates. We like to call it turning lemons into lemonade.'

Using social media usefully and authentically

As well as being a strong advocate and early adopter of SMS, Hugh loves to play with the power of social media. Ugly invest a lot of time connecting with their audiences on emerging platforms like TikTok. Subsequently, it should not be a surprise that they over-index in support and awareness from the 18 to 25s. Hugh also uses his personal social channels to keep his followers updated with his latest thoughts and business progress.

> It's not trend marketing. It is just another way to connect with our audience. It is authentic. It's not scripted. I just post stuff that excites me. I think Ugly is cool, and I like sharing what we do. I want to inspire other people that they can start something off from their bedroom in London and end up launching in a retailer in Tennessee.

> Most importantly, I believe in what Tony Hsieh from Zappos said, 'a great brand is a story that never stops unfolding'.

> Sharing my story is another way to build our community. The buzz created on Twitter and LinkedIn has also helped us connect with investors, and we have raised millions of dollars through engaging on these platforms.

Putting customers before a quick profit

Overall, Hugh's success is that by making DTC and the internet his brand platform, he has a constant feedback loop informing him how to best serve his customers. For example, their subscription service is only there for the convenience of their customers rather than being a tool to maximize profits.

> Hooking people in and keeping them subscribed is a great business model. But as a consumer-centric marketeer, I'm always thinking about what's most convenient for the customer. For me, the most important thing is to keep customers engaged and excited and for us to understand what they want. We offer subscriptions but make it super easy for customers to order more, less, pause or cancel. SMS is great for doing this. Our customers can send a text and say, 'hey, we need more cans', we can then send them a message back, and they can order more from there. We also have email functionality where we can send an email to remind our customers that their subscription order is coming, and they can hit a link and amend it any way they want. We have learnt we need to be flexible and fluid, and our subscriptions are an amazing part of that.

Going glocal

What impressed me the most is the distinction Hugh makes between using the internet as a platform to reach everyone and how he connects to his customers in the most immediate way possible. It is a mindset Hugh calls 'glocal', which means global/local. Ugly is building an international brand with a decentralized team across the United States and the UK. However, once they connect to a customer or follower, they find ways to serve them as an individual. They tailor their interactions to tell each customer about local stockists and events, adapt to their preferences and are always on hand to hear what they think. This glocal approach is the platform for Hugh's longer-term vision. 'We see our future as being the Willy Wonka of sparkling water. We are going to be making more flavours, with more collaborations and more events. We are going to be innovating and creating stuff ahead of our competitors. We will continue to stick our tongue out and do things that other people can't.'

LESSONS FROM UGLY

1 While DTC provides low margins for a soda company, Ugly uses it as the marketing channel that powers the other 80 per cent of the business. DTC is also a powerful way of putting the consumer first. If a customer has a particular requirement, idea or problem, the DTC channel provides the best way to connect with the customer and react.

2 Ugly mitigates the high relative shipping costs by optimizing wherever they can. For example, they encourage customers to buy in bulk and use sales data to find the best location for their warehouses to minimize handling and delivery miles.

3 They use a remote team to build a global brand; however, they still have local touchpoints. For example, order control, customer service and brand building are remote. However, they use local resources and influencers for store visits and events. They also use their DTC data to tailor their communications to be relevant to where their customers live.

4 Using their DTC channel for exclusive limited editions creates excitement within their community, and it also acts as Ugly's research and development channel. The community helps select new flavours and validates them. The company can then use this knowledge to feed new flavours into their retail channels with more confidence.

5 Hugh and his team are always happy to embrace technology to connect with their customers. They champion social platforms like TikTok, Twitter and Instagram while also using email and SMS to allow personal, quick, fluid and flexible interactions with their community. Hugh also uses his personal social media profile to promote the business and connect with other stakeholders, including investors.

14

Overcoming the challenges of a frozen supply chain to accelerate an inevitable shift to plant-based diets

allplants

One of the common assumptions around DTC is that it is now possible to access any product via the DTC channel. And it is true, more or less. Just about every brand on the planet is trying to figure out how to serve its customers directly. We have learnt throughout this book that the key motivations to go direct are the informational advantages and the ability to create a more emotional connection. Brand owners are also keen that they do not miss out on sales to those consumers who prefer to buy online. While these benefits are clear, not all brands choose to offer a DTC service. For many, it's either too complicated or too expensive. One of the critical factors in complexity and cost is packing and shipping. Some products are just too awkward and or costly for home delivery. In these instances, the best and cheapest way to serve their customers is via traditional retail channels.

In the last chapter, we saw how Ugly drinks have had to work hard to mitigate the high relative shipping costs by being smart with their warehouse locations and pack sizes. Weight was their most significant issue, but an even bigger challenge is when the complexity of temperature control is required. In recent years we have seen many businesses who have figured out a way to deliver chilled products.

They include meal kit companies like Hello Fresh, Mindful Chef and Blue Apron. There are also several companies offering complete ready-made chilled meals like Freshly in the United States and Tastily in the UK.

The challenge of frozen food

Keeping products cool to avoid spoiling is difficult but achievable with some good insulation and cooling packs. Harder still is frozen food where an even lower temperature must be maintained. Keeping things very cold all year round is hard, and subsequently, it is expensive. For this reason, there are not many DTC frozen businesses around, and successful frozen DTC strategies are rare. One of those exceptions is London-based allplants, a vegan frozen food business.

The company now delivers around 50,000 meals every week from Europe's biggest plant-based only kitchen. Co-founder and CEO Jonathan Petrides, known to all as JP, led me through his story and how he navigated the complexities of introducing a new brand into a nascent category with a product that is prepared by hand, flash-frozen, then stored and delivered still frozen.

How big family meals fostered a love and respect for food

JP is a foodie and a social entrepreneur, to the point that running a vegan food company almost seemed inevitable. Inevitable maybe, but his journey to get there was not straightforward. JP was raised in a half Cypriot, half Welsh household in North London. In 1974 when Turkey abruptly claimed ownership of North Cyprus, his father and his family lost everything and were forced to flee the country as refugees. Eventually, his dad found his way to London, where he had been due to study hospitality and use that education back in Cyprus. With a new life in England in mind, his focus shifted from tourism and hospitality to accountancy and management. In his first year at university, he also met his wife and shortly after, the new couple set up home in London, having three children, with JP being the oldest. I mention this because being from a Greek Cypriot family was to have a lifelong influence on JP and his siblings, particularly regarding their love of food, mealtime and cooking. Food was an essential part of growing up. Large traditional Greek family meals were a key feature in the Petrides house. JP explained, 'Food is very much core to our culture and big meals and mezes consisting of lots of meat, fish and dairy are the Greek way. I've very much not been brought up as veggie.' The conversion to vegetarianism and then becoming a vegan would come later.

JP did well at school and, like most of us, did not have much of an idea of what should come next. After university, he dabbled with banking (he liked the money but not the culture), then accountancy, which he liked even less. Eventually, he decided he wanted to be a management consultant. The challenge with consultancy is that the top firms tend to select the best of the academic best. While JP was no slouch, he was a long way from the academic elite. What he had on his side was tenacity and the ability to learn.

> No one from Nottingham University is supposed to go to McKinsey, but I found a way. First, I applied to every small consultancy firm I could find and ended up doing something like 60 interviews. If you practise enough, you get very good at this sort of interview. And so it was when the McKinsey interview came round I managed to ace it. It's similar to the early days of our first fundraising efforts when early meetings are always terrible, but then you get better and better at it.

The evolution of a social entrepreneur

Being a management consultant gave JP access and experience in a wide range of industries, including telecoms. It was while he was doing his work at McKinsey that he discovered the book *Creating a World without Poverty* by Nobel Peace Prize winner Muhammad Yunus, which outlines how it is possible to eliminate global poverty using collateral free microloans. The book had a tremendous influence on JP, and he became determined put these ideas into action. Using Yunus' plan as inspiration combined with his background in telecoms, he was fascinated by the opportunity to use mobile phones to provide a safe way to save and borrow money in the developing world.

> I became obsessed and realized that there was an opportunity. In Africa, everyone had a mobile phone, but very few had a bank account. It was now possible to use mobile payments to bank the unbanked. So I did this crazy thing of moving to Kenya, having never set foot in Africa, to build a mobile bank.

Teaming up with other telecom evangelists to found this idea, JP and his co-founders managed to get a small grant from the World Bank to build their app and prove its viability.

> We had managed to hack together an app using SMS technology and via the grant had enough money to set up nano loans for about 250 people. It was chaos, and no one thought it would work, but when about 90 per cent of the people paid back their loans within a month and were looking for further financing, we realized we were doing something important.

It was not easy – it took three years to get regulatory approval and required shutting down the whole business and starting again – but the mobile banking app idea worked. Within a month of the full launch, the company had a million users, and within three months, 6 million users. Today, the product, M-Shwari, is still thriving, serving over 20 million active users across East Africa. After a few years of growing and refining the service, JP decided to step down. However, that was not the end of his African social entrepreneurial adventure. With a group of friends he had met while in Kenya, this time, JP turned his hand to healthcare and co-founded his second business with the vision to become Africa's most trusted healthcare provider. The critical insight the team had was from interviewing 1000 women. 'The finding was 80 per cent of people were explicit that they would not go back to the last place they got healthcare because it was so bad. When there is no relationship or trust, providing preventive care and education is impossible.' The vision to become East Africa's most trusted healthcare provider came to pass, and the business now has over 650 employees and 27 clinics across Nairobi with plans to roll out across Kenya and into Nigeria. JP remains a shareholder and cheerleader but is no longer actively involved. He had spent five years in Africa and was ready to return to the UK and build something closer to home.

Returning home with a new ambition

In his late 20s and back in the UK, JP started to brainstorm new business ideas. His first thought was to use his experience from Africa to build a modern Western business in a new way. He thought about setting up a new mobile bank (think Monzo before Monzo) and dabbled with ideas to revolutionize the NHS. Although they were big and exciting ideas, he had not yet found something he was willing to commit to. 'I realized that I could never build these things unless I could see myself committing to them for the next 10 to 20 years. They are difficult ideas, and unless you are willing to run through brick walls on a daily basis, there is no point.'

The penny dropped for JP when he started dating a girlfriend (now his wife) who was a vegetarian. Eager to impress, he started making exclusively vegetarian meals at home. Still, he explained how she had yet to fully convert him.

> While I was like this is great, and of course, we can do this [eat
> vegetarian food] at home, I still had this kind of idiot belligerent male
> persona. And I would be trying to eat as many steaks and burgers as
> I could every time I was out with friends. Things really changed around
> 2015, when I started seeing some really powerful documentaries
> about the damage the animal agriculture industry was having on the
> environment. It really captured my imagination and helped me join
> the dots. I realized that although I always thought of myself as an
> environmentalist, the way I was eating was completely misaligned with
> my intentions. I felt like a massive hypocrite. The more I understood

the problem, I became convinced that it was imperative that we need to change the way agriculture works. The move away from meat, fish and dairy was inevitable. What was not so inevitable was the speed we were going to get there. The final piece of the puzzle was when also at the very same time my brother Alex called me up and mentioned he was now vegan. That pushed me over the edge, and my plant curious adventure began.

Frustrations due to the accessibility of a good plant-based diet

Once fully committed to a plant-based diet, JP found how hard it was to maintain. He explained:

> Eating plant-based food turned into a massive passion and a hobby. I was cooking like crazy for the first three or four months, figuring out how to make this change without it having to be a massive compromise. I wanted to be convinced that the food could be delicious. When I had the time to cook, I totally succeeded. However, when I became busy again, it became really hard. I was having to skip meals and eat carrots and hummus three nights a week as restaurants and supermarkets had zero options. The other thing I noticed was that my friends were really sceptical of my new diet. No amount of reason or science could convince them. The information did not cut through. The only thing that would change their minds is when I started to ask them to eat the food I was cooking, and they'd be like, 'wow, and you're telling me there is no meat in that?' Proving vegan food could taste great was the answer. And after that revelation, I was on a mission to try and accelerate this massive social movement. I had no idea how I would do it, but I knew this was the thing I could spend the next couple of decades on.

The first idea to accelerate the plant-based movement was to open some restaurants. The concept would be a 100 per cent plant-based, upmarket, quick-serve restaurant like Leon in the UK and Sweetgreen in the United States. This idea was shelved when JP discovered how much capital is needed to open up a chain of restaurants. Due to its lower entry costs and national reach, DTC was a more attractive option, but the format was still the issue. JP wanted to make sure that there were as few barriers as possible to converting to his plant-based food.

Meal kits, like Hello Fresh, were viewed by JP as, 'entertainment that was unlikely to result in long-term commitment for the majority of people'. Chilled ready meals, like Freshly, were seen as too much of a commitment as JP was aware that many customers would not want to eat exclusively meat-free and did not want to burden people with a fridge full of food that might go to waste. The objective was to convince customers that vegan food did not have to be a compromise or a hassle.

Using frozen food to achieve quality and flexibility

The answer then was frozen.

> We wanted to create something of mind-blowingly good quality that would enable us to build a new category. We also wanted to provide for people who were not going to go vegan overnight but were willing to try a couple of times a week or even a couple of times a month. Frozen reduces food waste and takes the pressure off as you had more than a few days to eat it. And frozen is the healthiest way to naturally preserve food. We can cook like you were at our restaurant, use natural quality ingredients and flash-freeze in all that nutrition and taste without needing preservatives. What's more, we knew frozen was seen as a premium category elsewhere in Europe, so we knew we could make good food this way.

Going frozen was sure to cause some manufacturing and delivery challenges. However, the first task was to see if there would be any demand for the idea. JP spent the whole of the spring and summer of 2016 in the kitchen. During that time, he also convinced his brother Alex to become his co-founder. To test his creations, JP had set up a Tuesday night supper club. 'We had a six-month product development period, fuelled by our supper club feedback. By the end of that, we had six recipes that were good enough to validate demand. By good enough, we meant a comprehensive range which we wanted people to taste.'

With a launch range ready, a Shopify website complete with a hand-drawn logo was cobbled together. JP had settled on 'all plants' as a project name from the start without realizing it would eventually become their brand. 'The name was there very early on. It was easy because whatever we did was all about plants.'

The market test

The challenge now was to see if there was any actual demand for their plant-based frozen meals.

> There were three of us, me, Alex and Ellie, our first hire. We pressed launch on the website and posted that it was live on our personal Facebook pages. It was the end of September, and we made 150 delivery slots available from then until Christmas. That was on a Friday, and by the time we came back together on Monday, we were sold out. Even more amazing was that most of the orders had come from people we did not know. Our Facebook post had been shared around, and we had sign-ups from all over the country.

With orders secured, the team then had to get busy. They set about doing the cooking, packing and labelling needed to use couriers to deliver the orders. As well as seeing if they could make the products, the big test was to see if the meals would arrive intact and at the right temperature. The secret to cracking the frozen challenge was lots of insulation (more on that later) with lots of testing by sending the meals to various addresses and using temperature probes to verify the sub-zero temperature could be maintained.

The final test was whether anyone would come back.

> We wanted to find out if we could get the nuts and bolts to work. It really gave us confidence because you only have a narrow set of proof

points in the early days. The first question was, was anyone going to buy it, and the second one was to check how many people would come back for a second order. We were not yet a subscriptions business, so it was just one-shot orders. When around 15 per cent came back in the next couple of months and to order again, it gave Alex and me the confidence to take all the savings we had ever had and pour them into the rent and kitting out our first proper kitchen. We then spent all our time cooking in the kitchen through October, November and December and launched officially on January 1st 2017.

Veganuary

The January launch date was significant. January was the month of the 'Veganuary' campaign. Veganuary is a charity that encourages the switch to a plant-based diet. The charity operates year-round with Veganuary, its flagship campaign, much like how Movember became an annual event for promoting awareness of men's health issues. 'Until we launched, the only brands Veganuary had to partner with were old-school vegetarian brands like Quorn and Linda McCartney. We had no money to spend on marketing, but I had become friendly with the team behind Veganuary, and they were incredibly support- ive.' This support extended to featuring allplants in their magazines and on their website.

> That's how the word got out despite our lack of marketing budget. We thought this was great, even though we did fear it would mean our customers would be in the 1 per cent of the population who were strictly vegan. That did not matter as we knew we could build the love there, and it would give us time to master our food and figure out how to reach the mass market. It was a pleasant surprise then when, at the end of that first year, we worked out that 60 per cent of our customers were not 'vegan' or 'veggie' at all. Our customers were mostly normal people trying to reduce their meat intake, eat more healthily and looking for an easy way to do this.

Raising money to expand

That first year was critical for the business. They had proved they could attract and maintain customers. They were also learning what it took to run a commercial kitchen, managing a variety of recipes and gaining supply chain and order expertise within the constraint of a frozen end product. The demand and expertise was enough evidence to raise a Series A round of £7.8 million (a record at the time, for a European vegan company). This money was to help the business find more customers and provide the capital to expand their operation.

allplants are another example of a vertically integrated organization (building in-house operations rather than outsourcing to others). Like graze and other businesses that operate this model, the benefits are clear; however, the advantages must heavily outweigh the additional set-up costs and risks.

JP is adamant that this is the right approach for them.

> We were told from the start that being frozen was a bit crazy, it's capital intensive, it's really hard, and there are loads of risks involved. However, from the beginning, I knew that if we were to be really committed to this, we needed to make a product 10× better than anything that had previously existed. This meant we could not outsource. If we are going to be the future of food, we have to be the people making the product because we know we need to be able to iterate and improve on a daily basis. This is the only way we could achieve our break out quality. The quality we achieve comes because we hand cook each recipe.

Building demand by turning customers into brand ambassadors

The capital secured has enabled them to build up their food manufacturing capability. To then justify that investment, they also needed to build more demand. JP told me his approach to acquisition and retention.

> The first thing to know is that when it comes to top-level brand awareness, we have barely invested anything into that yet. What we

have done is appeal to particular needs and allow our customers to be our ambassadors to spread the word. At the moment, the most important thing to us is that we are part of conversations that our customers have with their friends and family. When someone hears about us, we then want to make it as easy as possible for them to make the choice to buy us or simply learn more about the journey into eating more plants. We have thousands of helpful articles on our website covering off every aspect of plant curiosity. We know people are looking for answers, so we want to make sure we provide information that is easy to understand and also make it fun. Most importantly, we want to provide the information in a friendly and relatable way, not to be preachy or judgemental. We want to move away from the vegan 1.0 style, which was always a bit like, 'Okay, I get it, but why are you wagging your finger at me?' Instead, our style is to make it fun, engaging and inclusive.

We also make the first visit to our website a really straightforward experience. While we now have hundreds of options on our menu, we don't want to bombard someone with this selection on their first visit. They would be like, 'Woah, I just got here, chill out'. So instead, we take them through an onboarding process where depending on their answers to some simple questions, we will curate them a set of recommended meals to get started.'

Continually innovating and improving to encourage customers to keep coming back again and again

The company has come a long way from those initial six meals at launch. The expansion into so many meals and product choices is about retention.

To get customers to come back again and again, we need to make the whole process exciting and delightful. The most important part of this is quality and innovation. We can send out many emails and offers, but the product is ultimately what it is all about. We are always constantly listening to what our customers do and don't like. When we know what they like, we can offer them even more products we have confidence they will enjoy. In this way, we continue to innovate and keep our kitchen living and breathing. The kitchen is something that is alive and not just a factory pumping out the same thing, week in, week out.

The company is committed to improving and innovating to better match its customers' tastes and habits. They are also meeting the challenges beyond the immediate needs of taste and health. When allplants first started, the main reason for choosing vegan food was for the health benefits. Animal welfare and the environment were also important motivations, but health was the most common reason for choosing a plant-based diet. Today, motivations are starting to change with concerns about the environment prompting more customers to get turned onto the brand because of their environmental conscience. Fortunately for the brand (and the planet), sustainability has always been core to its mission.

Committing to a triple bottom line

The first thing JP did when he incorporated the company was to change the standard articles of association, a legal document that all businesses have that specifies the regulations for a company's operations and defines the company's purpose. Most companies use a boilerplate template that states that the directors in the business will behave sensibly and legally to maximize profits for their stakeholders. A focus on profit alone did not match the aims of allplants, which is why JP used the articles associated with a B Corp or public benefit corporation from the very start.

B Corps are certified to have a social and environmental purpose built into their internal processes and business goals. To become a B Corp, there is a rigorous set of audited requirements that a business is assessed against. Most importantly, any B Corp must commit to being more than a business focused on profit alone. The most common way to describe these integrated and expanded targets is to have a triple bottom line consisting of profits, people and the environment. Being a B Corp does not mean you don't want to make money. What it does do is ensure you have additional practices and processes in place to protect externalities like social welfare and the global environment. Famous examples of B Corps include Patagonia, Ben & Jerry's, The Body Shop and innocent drinks.

Being a B Corp is a big commitment. It limits what you do, whom you work with and even who can invest. It also requires lots of ongoing administration to prove that you are keeping your standards up to scratch. Becoming a B Corp is hard and an impressive achievement for any business. For allplants, even if they had to wait for their official certification, a B Corp structure was deemed critical from Day One. Committing to the B Corp methodology sent a signal to potential investors and customers about their businesses and what they stood for.

As well as good governance, sustainability is at the heart of every allplants product. JP explained:

> One of the things I discovered when I went into my research rabbit hole in 2015 was that food has a major impact on a person's carbon footprint. Today food accounts for over 30 per cent of global carbon emissions. I also discovered that food choices around sustainable packaging and transportation make only a small difference. What really makes the difference is what you put on your plate. Meat, fish and dairy are the biggest problems, and if you go fully vegan, it is about an 85 per cent reduction of the carbon footprint associated with your food choices. Our mission is about helping people understand this and accelerating the adoption of more plant-based meals.

The company also does all it can to ensure its production and deliveries are as sustainable as possible. Delivering frozen packages is a difficult thing to do. It requires storage and assembly in sub-zero temperatures. To minimize their logistics burden, allplants now operate their picking and packing from a site next to the depot they use for their outbound deliveries.

Of course, the biggest challenge is how to keep the product frozen from when it leaves the warehouse to ending up in your freezer via your doorstep. To do this, they have consistently improved on their packaging. They continually iterate on delivery materials like cardboard boxes and their insulation. Dry ice keeps the temperature down, and upcycled cotton fibres are wrapped around the product to keep them cold. The problem remained how much insulation was required. 'We were using so much insulation and had put so much effort into getting it right. Then, I had this crazy idea. While we were encouraging our customers to recycle the insulation, it was also really expensive and material intensive to make. So I thought, recycling is okay, but we really should be reusing it. So what we did was put a return label in the box to pay for the postage and request our customers to send it back to us. It was just an experiment to see if anyone did it. In the first three months after we started with the return to sender labels, over 40 per cent of our customers were now sending back their insulation to the point we had to hire an additional warehouse unit to store them.'

The future for allplants and your plate

This attention to detail, which makes it all the easier to choose to switch to an allplants meal, has grown the business to over £12 million in annual revenues. At the time of writing, the business remains strictly DTC.

> We have retailers knocking on our door and have done a few experiments, but for now, we want to continue to supply directly. It means that we know every single household that has ever tried allplants. As well as knowing who they are, we also get constant feedback from these customers to help us work out what we should make next.

While there seems to be plenty of headroom in the current DTC model, focusing on DTC only makes sense. However, the business is now also well equipped to start to think about moving in multiple directions. In October 2021, the company announced it had raised a £38 million Series B.

I agree with JP that the change to eating more plant-based meals is inevitable. If you have not already converted to a more plant-based diet, expect that to change. It is also highly likely that allplants will be a brand that helps you with your own plant-curious journey.

LESSONS FROM ALLPLANTS

1   Learning your trade. JP showed the benefits of building his experience and expertise. He was able to get a job at the top consulting firm McKinsey, but only after dozens of interviews with other consulting companies. He then learnt how to run a business by setting up social impact-oriented ventures in Africa before starting allplants. JP also demonstrates the importance of doing your homework for both knowledge and inspiration. His connection to Muhammad Yunus' book took him to Africa. Then a deep dive into the impact of veganism on the environment convinced him of the importance and inevitability of a plant-based future.

2   Letting the product do the convincing. JP found out that if he wanted people to follow in his footsteps and adopt more plant-based choices, lecturing them on the benefits is of little use. Inbuilt biases and cynicism means that no amount of logic and information is a match for actually tasting the product and proving that it does not have to come with a compromise

3   A solid market test. JP and his brother initially had just six meals, no marketing budget and 150 delivery slots to test their concept. Despite these limitations, they were able to verify their ability to acquire customers, retain them and operate a frozen supply chain. They needed to prove all these things before they had enough confidence in a full launch.

4   Marketing with no marketing budget. The brand immediately connected with an audience via the Veganuary campaign. Better still, they could do this without a huge marketing budget as Veganuary wanted to promote more ways for its supporters to access more plant-based meals. Finding a partner with a shared goal was a brilliant win-win for both businesses.

5   allplants are obsessed with making things as easy as possible for their customers. Choosing frozen meals gave maximum flexibility to their customers to eat the products whenever they choose. Unlike other DTC food businesses, following a regular schedule or commitment to enjoy the products is not required. The website's design is not to overwhelm new customers with too many choices. Furthermore, there are no wagging fingers or guilt trips, just friendly and accessible guidance, information and FAQS.

6   They committed to sustainability from Day One. Writing B Corp articles into the business from inception signalled what type of business the company wanted to be, helping it connect with the right customers and investors. It also meant it was easier for the business to get its B Corp certification as soon as it could. The company is also always looking for ways to be more sustainable. A great example is setting up a system to reuse the insulation needed to keep the products frozen. Closing this loop is both more environmentally conscious and also reduces cost.

15

How DTC is helping a whole town get its mojo back

Hiut Denim

David Hieatt is the co-founder of Hiut Denim, a premium jeans company he set up with his wife, Clare. Hiut is an abbreviation of Hieatt + Utility. Clare is actually the boss as she owns a fractionally bigger slice of the business than David. But I met with David as he makes a living by telling stories. And the story he told me is how he uses DTC and his keyboard to stay in complete control of his destiny. And his mission? To give a Welsh town its mojo back.

A maker and maverick

David has impeccable entrepreneurial credentials. He is a college dropout (actually, he was kicked out). He then travelled to London with no money or experience and bagged himself a job with Saatchi & Saatchi as an advertising copywriter. From there, he would eventually co-found, each time with Clare, three of the most acclaimed and creative brands in the UK: Howies, The Do Lectures and Hiut Denim.

What makes David different from other successful founders is that he is a somewhat reluctant entrepreneur. The classical definition of an entrepreneur is an individual who creates a new business, bearing most of the risks and enjoying most of the rewards. It is true that he starts businesses but is not into taking big risks (the stakes are too high for that), and any reward is to be shared, not hoarded. Rather than entre-preneur, David is better described as a branding expert, philosopher and coach. He is also a maker of great products and a master of communications, with his chosen medium being the internet.

The making of a maverick

David's interest in branding and communication began when, as a teenager, he stumbled across a copy of *On Advertising* by David Ogilvy. In that book was the observation that in the creative depart-ment of an advertising company, you don't need qualifications, but you needed ideas. For someone full of ideas and ambition but with-out a degree and who 'couldn't even spell at the time', this sounded like somewhere he belonged. It took David 18 months to land a job in advertising. But it was worth the wait when he landed a role with one of the most prestigious advertising agencies in the world: Saatchi & Saatchi.

The next few years were learning about the power of branding and communication, but then something big happened at Saatchi, which would put David on the path to Howies and eventually Hiut. In 1993 Robert Louis-Dreyfus, then CEO of Saatchi & Saatchi, bought the sportswear giants Adidas. For David, this was great. He loved sport and loved sports brands even more. Unfortunately, what happened next was that Louis-Dreyfus had fallen out with the Saatchi brothers, Maurice and Charles. So rather than going with Saatchi & Saatchi, he awarded the Adidas advertising contract to upcoming rivals, Leagas Delaney.

By this time, David was completely obsessed with writing ads for the Adidas contract and rather than losing out on the chance, he took a pay cut and went to work for Leagas Delaney instead. He then did spend the next few years writing ads for Adidas; however, his bosses decided his creations were not the voice they wanted for the brand. Despite this, David knew what he had been creating was an essential take on the sports clothing industry and was something worth sharing. So he took that voice and started writing slogans for t-shirts. Then, to sell and distribute the shirts, he and Clare created Howies as a side project.

From side project to Carnaby Street

Howies began in 1995 using David's ideas to design t-shirts for people like him who were into niche outdoor sports like BMX, mountain biking, skateboarding and surfing. T-shirts with slogans like 'Work Hard, Canoe home' and 'Porridge – The Breakfast of Champions' started appearing on the streets, skateparks and trails. Howies remained a side project until 2001 when David and Clare left London and headed back to their native Wales to work on Howies full time. They ended up setting up shop in Cardigan on the West Coast of Wales. It is a beautiful, if not remote, place to set up a business. However, being remote was not a problem for Howies. They made most of their sales via their beautifully designed home order catalogues and were also starting to figure out e-commerce. Besides being surrounded by hills, woody trails and surf also inspired the brand and reminded them what they stood for.

Howies was remarkably successful. Sales grew and grew, as did the team and products. In addition to t-shirts, the brand also sold jackets, underwear, sweaters, bags, trousers and, crucially, jeans. In addition to mail and web orders, they also started selling their products wholesale and even opened a Howies store on London's iconic Carnaby Street.

Storm clouds over the town

For Howies, business was booming. However, down the road, something less inspiring was happening. Cardigan was also where the UK's biggest jean manufacturer was based. The Dewhirst jeans factory regularly turned out 35,000 pairs of jeans a week and had been doing so for three decades. To say the factory was essential to the town is an understatement. Cardigan is a town of about 4000, and the jean factory employed 400. So when in 2002 the announcement was made that the factory would be closing (its biggest customer had chosen to source cheaper jeans from Morocco), it was a hammer blow for the town. David described it as:

> like watching a car crash in slow motion. When the factory shut bit by bit, the town started to lose its mojo. Shops started closing, one by one. Pubs went from being full on a Friday to almost empty. The town had entered a period of decline. Farming was still important, as was tourism, but a town cannot hope that by being busy for six weeks, that it will get through the year.

The other thing for David to contend with was that this was not the first time he had seen this happen.

> When I was growing up in the [South Wales] Valleys, on the bus on the way to school each morning, I saw the miners heading off with their little sandwich tins. Then on the way home, I saw them again. They would have just been coming out of the pits, with blackened faces and empty sandwich boxes. And then, one day, they were just not there. We were from a mining community. My grandfather was a miner, Clare's grandfather was a coal miner. Coal mining was not only the main industry of our town. It was the main industry for South Wales. When the pits closed, it was all desperately sad. I saw for the first time what happens when an industry changes and started to understand the importance of economics and the power it has on the community.

When growth becomes too much of a good thing

While it was tough times for the town they had made home, David and Clare had their hands full managing Howies while it continued to scale and scale. 'We hadn't really run a business before and were pretty naive.' Still, they must have been doing something right with suitors wanting to buy the company, including Steve Case, founder of

AOL and PPR (owners of Gucci and Yves Saint Laurent). It was fortunate that they were able to attract these sorts of offers as rapid growth had come at a price. David and Clare had already mortgaged their house twice to raise the capital the business needed to keep up with growth. Yet even then, more money was required to buy stock and service debt. It was at this point that David and Clare started listening to offers. The business was up for sale, but they would only partner up with a company that would continue to support and nurture their outdoorsy and environmental spirit. In the end, they agreed that the outdoor clothing company Timberland was the best fit for the brand. So in February 2007, it was publicly announced that Timberland now owned Howies, with David and Clare remaining in charge to take the brand onto the next level.

You would have likely heard this part of the story before. Founders sell their business. Those founders stick around to continue to run the business but don't like the fact they have lost control and do not see eye to eye with the new owners. The founders then quit the company they started. Of course, there is always more to any story than a straightforward narrative. For Howies, throw in the global financial crisis of 2008. But the result was the same: by 2009, after 14 successful years, David and Clare had walked away from Howies.

Starting again

The couple needed a break. Not that they were not doing anything in this period. They were busy making a new home for their young family in an old farmhouse located just outside the town. And it was from there that they launched the Do Lectures, an event hosted in their barn. The Do Lectures is an annual phenomenon, bringing together talks from some of the most creative and inspirational minds around. Speakers have included Tim Berners-Lee, Maria Popova, Michael Sheen, Ellen Bennett and Tim Ferriss. Think of the Do Lectures as a more humble, natural, intimate TED talks event. Only 100 people can attend as that's the capacity of the barn. But it's an event for everyone as those 100 in-person tickets pay for putting all the talks online, free to view. Some of these talks have now been seen more than 150 million times.

The Do Lectures provided the opportunity for David to teach; however, he is also a maker. When he had introduced jeans to the Howies range, he had become a complete denim head, learning about the history, materials, processes and equipment needed to separate a quality pair of jeans from the also-rans. David knew he wanted to start a jeans brand. Yet, he hesitated.

Searching for the 'why'

I wrote the business plan for Hiut, which was to make the best jeans in the world in 2010. I also had investors saying, 'great, let's do this', but I put it on the back burner. I was beaten up and felt deflated. At the time, I was not thinking about the town, and therefore the idea got parked. I just couldn't work out why I wanted to run around the same track twice. Instead, I was running up the hills with my dog, shouting and screaming, getting slightly angry, and I did that for a year. Then one day, I had a call from Gideon, our jeans designer, who said, 'Why aren't you doing the plan? It's a great plan.' I told him how I was not sure why I would want to run around the same track twice, and I still had some scars from Howies. He then said, 'Well David, it's not really about you. I thought it was about getting the town making jeans again.' That was the lightning bolt moment. I was like, oh, that's why I want to run around the track twice. It's not about me. It's about the town. We are going to get 400 people their jobs back.

David now had his why.

I had the energy now. I remember the coal miners' faces. I have seen the town boarded up and the empty pubs. I did not want to see that movie again. I knew that even if it was a ridiculously silly dream of getting the 400 jobs back, I am happy to fail if failure was only getting 30 people their jobs back. Even if we don't get to 400, we would still be a town of makers, and we would have still passed skills on. So even failure is pretty good.

A unique period of time

Central to the plan of getting the town to make jeans again was using DTC and the internet. There were to be no stores, no wholesalers and no retailers. Hiut would use the internet to trade and find customers.

> DTC was important because the economics worked. We could tell our stories using the motorways in the skies. Whether it was Twitter, Facebook or Instagram, we could send our stories all over the world for very little money. We knew the better we were at telling our story, the more people would find out about us. We were in a special period of time; the town had these unique skills, we had learnt how to build a brand, and the internet had happened. It was a convergence of being able to make, tell the story and having the internet to spread the word. This convergence meant we had the wind at our backs rather than blowing in our face.

Getting the band back together

David and Clare's first job was to recruit back the people who had the skills and knowledge to make their jeans. The secret was locating the sample machinists.

> The sample machinists are quite rare because while everyone else was a cog on a production line, the sample machinists were the grandmasters who knew how to make a finished jean from head to toe. There were about six sample machinists whom we had to track down. They had each spent 20,000 or 30,000 hours on learning their craft. Finding them was the first time I was surrounded by people with absolutely the highest level of skills. They were perhaps the best jean makers in the world.

When the Dewhirst factory was shuttered, the workforce had scattered, as they had to look further afield for a job. The grandmasters had spent the last 10 years doing anything other than making jeans. One was working in a pub, another was selling trousers in Marks &

Spencer and one was even working in a shoe factory in London. 'This was grandmaster Elin. She hated it and hated London. She was a denim girl.' Once they had been found, it did not take long to convince the grandmasters, the former sample machinists, that Hiut would turn Cardigan back into a jean-making town, and they signed up to make the dream come true.

Staying in control

Meanwhile, David was still sore from what happened at Howies and determined that it would be different this time.

> I had learnt that if we grew too fast, that was dangerous. I learnt from Howies that things soon get out of control when that happens, and the business needs more and more money. We prefer slower growth as it gives us the chance to be in control of the business. If we can self-fund ourselves, we can be in control. Staying independent matters. It may be counter-intuitive because we could easily grow the business faster by making t-shirts and servicing lots of wholesale accounts. But I have learnt that stuff also makes us super vulnerable. If we don't maintain control, our business could be taken to China or wherever to make better margins. This business is about the people in the factory. They have heard the thunk of the gates closing once. My job is to make sure that never happens again. I have to save us from my impatience and choose the harder route up the mountain. But choosing the hard way also makes us strong, tough as hell.

Maintaining independence had been embedded in the structure of the business from the start. Hiut has only had one investment round, and that was right at the beginning. Their investors have a stake, but their shares have no voting rights (voting shares are kept only by David and Clare), there are no dividends as all profits are put back right back into the business, and they should expect to be in for the long term as there is no exit plan.

Being responsible even if the answers are imperfect

It has worked. After nine years, Hiut remains fiercely independent and in control of its growth. David is content with progress.

> The team is now up to 30 people. I don't worry about our size, especially as I am a believer in the power of compound growth, where the biggest gains happen towards the end. For me, we have never been closer to 31 people, and the team is getting better every day. In the end, I know that it's going to compound, and we can be one of the most influential brands in the world with the lowest impact.

By lowest impact, David means that Hiut is doing all it can to be a sustainable brand.

> By making better quality jeans, we move away from regular jeans that don't last very long, use a tonne of water, all sorts of chemicals and an incredible amount of energy. But also our job is to recognize we are still a polluter. Because we make stuff, we will always be taking [from the earth] more than we give. We are not kidding anyone that this is a completely green jean, but everything we do is a step in the right direction. Using 10× less water, removing micro-plastics and offering free repairs for life are the right things to do, but we know it's still an imperfect answer.

The most impactful thing Hiut does in terms of the environment has nothing to do with the factory but by influencing the behaviour of the consumer. Each pair of jeans sold comes with the invitation to join the 'no-wash club'. To qualify, you need to resist the temptation to wash your jeans, ideally for six months. The rationale is it's better for your jeans (better colour and comfort) and better for the planet. Not washing your clothes is initially a hard sell but is made possible by the communication and community enabled by DTC. In addition to promoting the benefits of joining the no-wash club on the website, each pair of jeans also comes with a small booklet with instructions on how to wash and not wash your jeans. This sort of enhanced communication and community is just not possible when you buy a pair of jeans off the shelf. DTC also means that the company can keep waste to an absolute minimum as each pair of jeans is made to order or in very small runs.

Connecting with people via the motorways in the sky

Being a DTC brand means that David has had to develop further his craft of finding ways to connect with customers via 'the motorways in the sky'. Like its jeans, Hiut marketing content is always of the highest quality. Still, David has had to work hard to connect that content with an audience.

> When we launched, we had a lot of press. Everybody loved the story of David vs Goliath and our company giving the town its mojo back. We were very good at telling the story, and when we launched, we had already received about six months of orders. As we were the manufacturer, we then had to make the orders. There are two types of stresses, getting no orders and having too many orders. Both need to be addressed. So I made the decision to shut down the website for three months to find some more people and make the customers we do have happy. It seemed like a sensible plan, but three months later, when we turned the website back on, the press had gone, and everyone had forgotten about us. There were no new orders coming in.

The business had gone from one extreme to another. David had to work out how to sell his jeans without relying on other people to tell the story.

> This was the point where I realized that as a direct to consumer brand, I needed to build this company from my keyboard. I also discovered what was really working was our newsletters. We had only a tiny number of subscribers, yet about 80 per cent of our sales came through our newsletter links. I could see dribbles of orders from all the things we were spending our money on, it was obvious there was something wrong. I knew I needed to spend 80 per cent of my time on the newsletter. It was clear as day. The other thing which helped was that,

at the time, no one else cared about newsletters. They were all about getting their Instagram feed right. So I was like, great, you stick to that game, and we are going to build our business through newsletters.

Hiut really does make great weekly newsletters. I would encourage you to sign up even if you have little interest in jeans. Because the surprising thing is, the newsletters contain very little news or conversations about jeans and denim. I questioned David why he did this.

The thing is, we don't have to give that much attention to our jeans. My view is that the type of customer interested in insanely well-made jeans is also likely to be interested in great design, great coffee and great architecture because that's the way a creative mind works. We see our customers in terms of a full 360 degrees. We see the whole of them. You can be a selvedge nut who is really into us, but that is only one segment of who our customer is. Talking about things other than us makes us a more interesting company and gives our customers more reasons to engage with us each week. When we write about craft beer, the best hotels and the like, we know because we have your attention the next time you think about purchasing a pair of jeans, you know what we stand for and are going to think of us first.

Being patient and ignoring the need for immediate results

David and his marketing team also spend thousands of hours writing blogs, tweets and long-form lists. They also annually produce a very limited edition printed yearbook. These yearbooks are a finely crafted and longer-form version of the stories, philosophies and characters that appear in the weekly newsletters. They also contain original stories and thoughts from David and his team, in addition to content from guest writers, photographers and illustrators.

The yearbooks are not only an advert for our jeans but our ethos. They allow us to have the best conversations with our customers. We make them so well we can send them to Jony Ive or whoever, and we know they will read them and not throw them away. Most brands are allergic to print as they only think about the costs. However, the print allows us to connect the digital world with the analogue, and I believe the best brands are combining those two things.

In this book, I have shared many examples of brands using data to better inform their decision-making. Seeing 80 per cent of sales coming from newsletters and then focusing on producing even better newsletters is an example of David doing the same. However, David also likes to rely on his marketing intuition. Because he has 25 years of brand building experience and believes in compound growth, he is prepared to start small and build, even when the data might be telling him to stop.

> As well as newsletters, the other thing we did is we created lists. The most important one is the yearly Do One Thing Well list. In the first year, I spent ages and ages on this list and like 27 people read it. But as I was a creative person, I thought it was important and just kept doing it. It was the same with the Makers and Maverick event [a mini one-day Do Lectures type event highlighting brands and people who share the same ethos for craft as Hiut] where it was tiny, and now it is a really important event for us. We now have people from Patagonia and all sorts of amazing people coming. And I am thinking, 'Wow, imagine if I stopped because I looked at the data.' The interesting thing is that people want immediate results, but if you want immediate results, you would never have any oak trees.

Meghan Markle and going home

David's approach to brand building is clearly working. Sharing the stories of Hiut and other makers and mavericks is making an impact on our culture. The best example of this influence is when the team received a phone call one Friday morning from Kensington Palace. Once an NDA had been signed, it was revealed that Meghan Markle had requested a specific pair of black Hiut jeans for an upcoming event. After scrambling to get them made and delivered to the Palace as requested, the phone began ringing off the hook three weeks later when Megan was spotted wearing her Hiuts. The brand was back in the news, and with it, three months of orders arrived overnight. Again David had the stress of more demand than the business could keep up with.

The size of their production unit was starting to hold them back. It was time to find a new home. They soon found the perfect spot. In 2018 they moved their equipment, materials and people into a bigger unit across town. Hiut had moved into the still vacant ex-Dewhirst factory. Jean making in Cardigan was now back where it had begun.

LESSONS FROM HIUT DENIM

1 David knew he was able to set up a jean company. He knew what it took to make a great pair of jeans and how to build a brand. Yet, he did not act until he had properly defined his 'why'. By focusing his energy and efforts to bring jobs back to the town, utilize and pass on the grandmasters' hard-won skills and ultimately bring the mojo back to the town, he had all the motivation he needed.

2 The Howies experience had taught David that while growth is good for business, too much growth can be a bad thing if it causes you to lose control. David vowed this would not happen to Hiut, especially as getting it wrong could lead to his team (and the town) losing their craft again. This time they would keep things in check with controlled growth, doing one thing well and relying on compound growth to make a long-term difference.

3 When David turned back on the website after the company was overrun with launch orders, he found that interest had waned. He knew he had to produce the content to connect with customers and discovered that his newsletters provided the best return. So rather than following current marketing conventions, he doubled down on newsletters and stopped spending time on what was not working.

4 David created a deeper level of engagement with his customers by not talking solely about denim and Hiut in his newsletters. Instead of treating their audience as one dimensional, providing a more varied and exciting conversation by talking about other interesting topics and brands means that they will gain and retain more newsletter subscribers.

What's more, when those subscribers want to buy their next pair of jeans, Hiut will be their first thought.

5 David is prepared to do it well and play the patient game to grow his business. It's the same story for Hiut's marketing. By being consistent and producing original and high-quality content, Hiut is building its influence even if the initial returns are low. The initial efforts of The Do One Thing Well lists, the Makers and Mavericks events and the yearbooks far outweighed the rewards. However, they persevered, and as their reputation grew, so did their audience, and today they are all key brand pillars.

Summing up

What are the rules of DTC?

So that's a wrap. If you follow the examples of the brands in this book, will you be guaranteed to replicate their success? Maybe, maybe not. But what should be clear is that if you do, you will have a considerable advantage over those who have not followed by their example.

Success depends on many variables, including many that are out of your control. Unfortunately, the reality of startups means that even if you follow every lesson in this book, you will still find launching a product via DTC a very uncertain enterprise. My intention has always been to unearth the knowledge to maximize the chances of a successful outcome.

If you plan to introduce a new product, the main takeout should be that DTC is the easiest and likely best route for you to get ideas to market. There has never been a better time to launch a product; barriers of entry are lower than ever and there is an endless selection of easy-to-access and easy-to-use tools available. And if you need help, for a fee, there is an army of advisors, agencies and freelancers on hand to steer you in the right direction. Of course, the problem with low barriers of entry is that competition has also never been greater. You will be far from the only one trying to serve your target customers. By studying the stories and applying the lessons highlighted in the preceding pages, the good news is that you will have a significant advantage over the rest.

Of course, your product needs to be up to scratch. It needs to be significantly better than what is currently available to make any impact. But remember, it's not just about the product itself. It's the way you can connect with your customers. It's how you provide them with what they need when they need it. Finally, it's how you build trust that you will continue to show up and make things a bit better every day.

Now that you have read the book, I am sure you will appreciate my comments at the very start about how hard it is to set rules when the landscape is evolving so rapidly. As demonstrated in the chapters on Cornerstone and Casper, intense competition and the ever-increasing cost of digital marketing means that simply relying on social media to acquire customers is not likely to be very efficient. While digital advertising remains an essential activity, it is an increasingly expensive way to build awareness and attract customers.

So before worrying about CAC and which social platforms to advertise on, instead here are the eleven main similarities shared by the best in class DTC brands in this book.

1 It is essential to **create a community** to serve and also to inform what you do and how you do it. Community is at the heart of the success of many brands in the book. TRIBE would not have started without its community of runners and athletes. Ugly keeps fresh and moving forward by providing new products and eliciting excitement and feedback from its drinkers. And the best example of the power and importance of the community came from Snag Tights, where the ingenuity and love from their community saved the business when it looked like it might run out of money.

2 To create a community, you must **have a strong brand**. Your brand is the outward representation of what you stand for. Once you have clarified who you are and what you care about, people who share your values will choose to connect with you. As a consumer, what you decide to buy is a representation of who you are. In the past, you may have signalled what type of person you are by the clothes you wear or the car you drive. Today it goes much deeper

with consideration about what brands people want to be associated with, going into each and every purchase. Connecting on an emotional level not only increases the likelihood of purchase, it also builds trust and loyalty, which drives repeat purchases and advocacy.

Recognizing that your brand is critical means that it cannot be an afterthought. A well-developed brand must be there right from the beginning. Lick and Clearing made sure they raised enough money to be able to afford to do comprehensive brand development before launch. That is one way. However, Hiut Denim also demonstrated how to build your brand without a marketing budget through consistency and quality via its newsletters, lists, yearbooks and events.

3 **At the heart of your brand must be your purpose.** Your purpose is why you get up in the morning and continue to show up day after day, even when things are not going well. We have seen how tails.com nearly fell at the first hurdle because while they had the near-perfect e-commerce set-up, they got into trouble as they had failed to work out what they stood for and to check what their customers expected from them. TRIBE's mission to eradicate modern-day slavery is the fuel for the whole business. It unites and motivates the team and also provides the stimulus for spreading the word. David Hieatt knew that defining the 'why' was critical before he started Hiut. The business could not begin without a reason and a purpose. That purpose also informed the parameters of their operation.

4 DTC brands are modern businesses. This modernity means they **do things differently** from what has come before. They are different because they know they need to be more nimble and innovative than their invariably better resourced competition. They are unafraid to try new things. For example, Who Gives A Crap has a novel 50/50 for profit/not for profit model and has insisted on a three-decade investment commitment. Ugly is using technology to facilitate a fully remote, globally distributed team. This model allowed Ugly to change its focus from the UK to the United States while continuing to serve both markets and retaining its team.

The companies I met are also committed to doing business more sustainably; they think carefully about the materials they use, their manufacturing processes, shipping techniques and even how they promote their products. With sustainability and social impact baked into their mission, it is no surprise that Who Gives A Crap and allplants are certified B Corps. However, so is graze, and I expect others in this book to follow their lead. These founders know their customers expect them to be responsible, and they are committed to finding ways to do business better.

5 These brands have also demonstrated that to build their reputation, increase retention and turn customers into advocates, **nothing is more important than customer experience** and customer service. DTC brands are famous for being obsessed with making sure customers are nothing less than delighted each time they receive an order. This obsession is why graze, tails.com, and allplants have built their own factories – they could not trust anyone else to do what they do.

Beyond manufacturing, every brand obsesses about how the product looks and gets from A to B. Late, damaged or unreliable deliveries are unacceptable. As Huel demonstrated, it is better to pay more than to let the customer down.

Finally, while all brands make it as easy as possible to buy and receive products, they know sometimes things will still go wrong. For this reason, they make it simple for customers to get in touch and ensure they quickly right any wrongs. For example, you won't get a job at Heights unless you can demonstrate an interest in the product AND a genuine joy of helping people. Best of all, they turn these conversations to their advantage, taking the opportunity to build relationships with their customers and finding out more about how they can serve them better. It's what Hugh from Ugly called 'Turning lemons into lemonade'.

6 **Gathering and using your data** is a prerequisite for all DTC brands and remains one of the key advantages over traditional retail lead businesses. Graze, allplants and Ugly use their review data to innovate and iterate their products. Bloom & Wild are obsessed with net promoter score. Snag Tights use customer data to inform their marketing, resulting in 10 per cent of their models being men, due to 10 per cent of their customers being male. What's more, Hiut also used sales data to show them that their newsletters were the source of customer purchases and not sexy Instagram ads.

7 Finally, DTC has proven to be time and time again **the best and easiest way to introduce a new product and provide a better service.** Without enjoying the low barriers to entry that DTC offers, Sugru and Who Gives A Crap would not exist. DTC has also allowed for better products and customer experience. Bloom & Wild, Lick, Casper, Clearing and tails.com all make products that would not make any sense without the ability to personalize and provide more satisfactory outcomes via direct deliveries.

While some of the businesses in this book remain DTC only, many have branched out into a more omnichannel/multichannel experience. Expanding into new channels was necessary for some brands as DTC alone could not provide the revenues they needed to thrive. For others, it was a way to grow, and for some, it was customer-driven. Omnichannel gives brands a way to meet their customers where they are and not expect them to always come to them. Omnichannel is an example of putting the needs of the customer first.

Another example of a customer-centric approach was Cornerstone removing the subscription-only default once they identified that, for some, subscriptions could be a more cumbersome and inconvenient experience than placing single orders.

While extending beyond DTC is usually good for growth, you need the know-how and resources to do it. Please also heed the cautionary tale of Sugru that highlights how not all channels work for all products.

Wait, there's more

These seven observations are a culmination of the insights shared during my interviews. When creating your own DTC offer, I recommend that you consider them all and omit any at your peril. While these seven behaviours are critical, there are also many other lessons in this book. Not every lesson or example will be relevant to your business, so the best approach is to mix and match and choose the ones that best fit your product, industry and ambitions. Also, remember these lessons are foundational thoughts, and the real work is in getting into the detail and rolling up your sleeves as you execute your vision.

Some thoughts on the interviews

My advantage going into this process was that I was a founder interviewing founders. That I was not a journalist or an academic meant that I could lean on my personal experiences to ask the most relevant and practical questions. It was also helpful that I could empathize with the founders as they recounted their motivations, struggles and successes. That I could relate directly with each founder resulted in long, open and honest conversations with the end result of more wisdom being shared. I also had a great time, and the stories and knowledge shared in these conversations exceeded expectations every single time.

All the founders had different personalities, and some were better at telling their stories than others. However, this did not matter, as actions speak louder than words. My job was to discover and record what they had done and why they did it. It was hard not to be impressed as I uncovered some formidable intellects, achievements and limitless drive. Whatever their background, I also realized that the critical thing they all had in common was the desire to help people and make a difference.

While having a degree from Oxford, having set up more than one business, being a technology whizz kid or branding expert will help, it is not the most important thing. The critical trait is the desire to provide something that does not currently exist and by doing so makes someone's life a bit happier and easier. The willingness to solve, improve and innovate gave Jane from Sugru the resolve to spend six years developing her product. Personal frustrations led Brie from Snag to create a better pair of tights. Likewise, Dan and Joel from Heights turned their personal struggles into a business with a mission to help others.

If you are equally motivated to create something new and use the rules and lessons in this book, you too can make a difference.

My one regret when writing this book was that I was not able to capture the stories of more female founders or founders with skin any other colour than white. The Western entrepreneurial world is still far too dominated by the privilege of middle-classe white men. I should know. I am one of them. As long as this trend continues, far too many sections of society will remain with problems that businesses like these should be solving. The difficulty we face is, it is easier and more motivating to solve a problem when you feel the pain yourself. Middle class white men do not have all the answers.

The good news is that DTC can be part of the solution. DTC provides the opportunity to start a new enterprise without the need for vast amounts of capital or risk. You can start small, and you can start at any time. What's more, there are also investors who are willing to back more diversity. The only requirement is to show that you have an exciting idea and the ability and dedication to make it happen. In this way, I hope this book can support the progress of levelling up by helping a more diverse wave of DTC entrepreneurs make their mark.

A NOTE TO THE READER

I have done my very best to accurately record and research the numbers, dates and events in this book to the best of my ability. I take full responsibility for any mistakes. I have attempted to tell the stories of the brands and founders as they were told to me. Hopefully, I have accurately captured the voice, spirit and meaning from these conversations. I apologize if anything was lost in translation; however, if this happened, I remain confident that the wisdom imparted will not have lost any of its authenticity or value.

As predicted, the brands in this story continue to grow and evolve. Since I penned the interviews, Lick have raised a substantial Series A. Bloom & Wild have absorbed two smaller competitors and expanded across Europe. Snag have introduced a range of clothes in addition to their tights and shorts. Anthony Fletcher has stood down from his role as CEO at graze, and it was announced that Casper is exiting Wall Street and will be taken private again.

I look forward to watching the further growth and evolution of all the trailblazers in this book, seeing what problems they solve next, and most of all I am excited about what more they have to teach us.

Don't be a stranger. Ask me any questions and let me know your ideas. You can find me at www.stevens.earth and on Twitter @openmikestevens.

Mike Stevens
Poole, England

ACKNOWLEDGEMENTS

First, thank you to all the founders and interviewees who took time away from building their businesses to chat with me and share their knowledge. Many of these interviews overran, and more than one required a second sitting, but not once did any of you hesitate, demur or deflect when asked one of my many questions.

Thank you to those businesses I spoke with but did not make the final cut. While I ultimately did not include these interviews, those conversations helped sharpen my game and immensely aided my knowledge. Thank you, Alessandro Savelli (Pasta Evangelists), James Cadbury (Love Cocoa and HIP chocolate), Rob Law (Trunki), Ilana Lever (Motley), Rhys Newman (Omata) and Dov O'Neil (Cubitts), for your contribution. Hopefully, I will get to share your adventures in DTC soon.

Thank you to my many friends and family for reading different drafts and chapters and for your continuous support. Special thanks in this regard go to Anna, Rio, Mike, Judy, Sasha and Lizzie.

This book would not have been possible without the support, encouragement and direction from the team at Kogan Page. Heather, thanks for your insightful feedback and advice and Chris, thanks for believing in me and guiding me through the somewhat antiquated art of publishing. Also, thank you, Sue Richardson, for the intro.

Big up to my former teammates at Peppersmith. I hope you recognize why I felt compelled to write this book and are satisfied I have uncovered some of the answers we spent so long trying to figure out. Dan, Dana, Lizzie, Sasha, Greg, Gracie, thank you for packing boxes, downloading orders, answering customer service calls, designing the website and packaging, finding suppliers, figuring out the software and for making too many to count trips to the post office, as we built our own little DTC empire. However, none of you could ever assemble a box as quickly as Abi. Abi, your records remain unbeaten.

Lastly, thanks to the unconditional support of my wife, Lou. If this book proves helpful, it is down to you. None of this would have happened if not for you.

INDEX

CPSIA information can be obtained
at www.ICGtesting.com
Printed in the USA
BVHW021722030522
636006BV00004B/59